S0-CBX-870

Limited Classical Reprint Library

THE

PROGRESS OF DOCTRINE

IN THE

NEW TESTAMENT,

CONSIDERED IN EIGHT LECTURES DELIVERED BEFORE THE UNIVERSITY OF OXFORD

ON

The Bampton Foundation,

BY

THOMAS DEHANY BERNARD, M.A.,

OF EXETER COLLEGE, AND RECTOR OF WALCOT.

WITH AN INTRODUCTORY NOTE BY

REV. T. W. CHAMBERS, D. D.

Klock & Klock Christian Publishers
2527 GIRARD AVE. N.
MINNEAPOLIS, MINNESOTA 55411

Originally Published by
American Tract Society
1896

Printed by Klock and Klock in the U.S.A.
1978 reprint

FOREWORD

In the early 1950s, soon after I had become a Christian, a friend of mine who was interested in my spiritual growth recommended that I buy a copy of Bernard's *Progress of Doctrine in the New Testament.* This work had recently reappeared on the book market after having been out-of-print and unobtainable for many years. I heeded my friend's counsel, bought a copy of Bernard's *Progress of Doctrine,* and savored his treatment of New Testament theology for several years before entering Dallas Seminary. There, in a course taught by none other than Dr. Charles C. Ryrie, author of the highly respected *Biblical Theology of the New Testament,* the study of Bernard's lectures was again recommended to me.

Thomas Dehany Bernard (1815-1904) was an English clergyman. He graduated from Exeter College, Oxford, and after several notable pastorates ministered at Wells Cathedral, ultimately becoming its chancellor. On three separate occasions he was selected preacher at Oxford, and in 1864 delivered his now famous lectures on 'The Progress of Doctrine in the New Testament.' These lectures were later published and the book went through several editions during the author's lifetime.

Thomas Bernard was noted for his strong evangelical convictions. While his activities included influential positions in civic, ecclesiastical and missionary organizations, he remained unfettered by 'party politics' and uncompromising in his adherence to the integrity of the Word of God.

It is a mark of the progress of time that I am now in the position of my friend who, nearly thirty years ago, recommended that I purchase a copy of Bernard's *Progress of Doctrine in the New Testament.* This is not an onerous task. In fact, I gladly recommend the purchase of this work knowing of the rich blessing which lies in store for the reader! I also trust that, in the providence of God, He will raise up men who, as with this noted English clergyman, will advance the cause of Christ!

-Cyril J. Barber

INTRODUCTORY NOTE.

THE Bampton Lectures of Mr. Bernard were first issued in 1864, and since that time have been continuously before the public, the work having been often reprinted both in Great Britain and America.

Its one theme, the "Progress of Doctrine in the New Testament," was by no means a novelty, but never before had it been presented in a popular yet lucid and convincing form. Hence the wide acceptance and great usefulness of the book. The present prominence of Biblical theology in the church's view has rather deepened than lessened the general interest in the subject. The Bible has more and more come to be regarded as the historical record of God's self-revelation to the children of men. As progress undeniably characterized the various stages of this revelation in the Old Testament, it was natural to expect the same in the New. And the fact of such progress has been generally admitted. It is true that the Lord Jesus Christ is the great revealer of God, and his life and teachings are faithfully recorded in the Gospels. But very much of the truth wrapped up in his person and work could not be fully explained and understood until after his death and resurrection, and especially after the outpouring of the Holy Spirit on Pentecost. The germs of the whole system were indeed uttered by him in the course of his ministry, but the disciples, even the Twelve, were slow of heart to comprehend. And the Master himself, as Mr. Bernard reminds us (p. 97), told them, "I have yet many things to say unto you, but ye cannot bear them now." Therefore he made provision, by sending the Paraclete, that these "many things" should not be lost, but subsequently put on record for the guidance and comfort of his people. The Acts, Epistles and Apocalypse contain this further disclosure of the Saviour's work and will, and so make the volume of revelation a complete, rounded whole, in which nothing is lacking. The agency of the Holy Spirit guarantees the accuracy of the writings of the Apostles, so that what they say is of equal validity with any utterances of the Lord Jesus. Oftentimes, indeed, it is of greater value, because it fully unfolds what could be given by him only in outline, or what was entirely withheld in view of the incompetency of the disciples to bear it.

It is the more important to have this point unfolded in the lucid discourses of Mr. Bernard, because in our day there is a pronounced tendency to overlook the Apostolic development of truth under the pretext of a return to Christ. But it may well be questioned if any man, no matter how endowed by nature or matured by grace, can get nearer to the heart of Jesus or be a more faithful mouthpiece of his views than Saul of Tarsus. It is true there are traces of his Rabbinical education in his writings, and these have sometimes been objected to as deteriorating the excellence and usefulness of what he says. But there is no possibility of separating these features from the rest of the Apostle's writings, and the inspiring Spirit must certainly have preserved him from any undue use of what he had learned before his conversion. On this point it is well to quote the words of the veteran scholar of Neuchatel, the acute and learned Prof. Godet, as given in his latest work, "Introduction to the New Testament" (p. 16). After referring to Pfleiderer's view of the rabbinical character of Paul's exegesis, both liberal and allegorical, and citing the cases alleged, he says, "I believe that in several of these cases Paul's explanation is fully justified (as Gal. 3:16; Rom. 4:17 and 10:6, *et seq.*), and that in other cases the typology of the Apostle entirely differs from the rabbinical allegories in this, that the two things compared by Paul always rest upon a common moral law that warrants the putting them together (1 Cor. 9:9; Gal. 4:21), while in the ordinary allegorical explanation the things brought together are so artificially, and only touch by an accidental feature. But I do not mean to say, notwithstanding, that a man who had not passed through the rabbinical gymnastics would have always argued as Paul does. Only it must be well observed that this was for him only a process of demonstration and not the means by which he had reached the very basis of his ideas. That basis he possessed before writing, and he the more willingly employed the Old Testament to defend it, that that was the authority his adversaries invoked against him: 'Ye that desire to be under the law, do ye not hear the law?' (Gal. 4:21.) It was a kind of argument *ad hominem*." To the same effect speaks Bishop Lightfoot (Galat. 196–7) concerning Paul and Philo's use of Hagar and Sarah: "Both allegorize and touch upon the same points in the narrative. Yet in their whole tone and method they stand in direct contrast, and their results have nothing in common. Philo is wholly unhistorical. With St. Paul, on the other hand, Hagar's career is an allegory, because it is a history. The symbol and the thing symbolized are the same in kind. This simple passage of patriarchal life represents in miniature the workings of God's providence hereafter to be exhibited in greater proportions in the history of the Christian church ... With Philo, the allegory is the whole substance of his teaching; with Paul, it is but an accessory. He uses it rather as an illustration than an argument, as a means of representing in a lively form the lessons before enforced on other grounds. It is, to use Luther's comparison, the painting which decorates the house already built."

In Fairbairn's "The Place of Christ in Modern Theology" occurs the following passage (p. 450): "We cannot accept Luther's article of a standing or a falling Church as our *principium essendi*. It is Paul's rather than Christ's; it may be true, but it still remains what it was at first—a deduction by a disciple, not a principle enunciated by the Master." Here there is a reversal of the view held by the historic church from the beginning, that the entire New Testament is the norm of faith, and that a distinct utterance by an inspired Apostle is as authoritative as one of our Lord's own sayings. Under the pretext of doing honor to Christ his own express teaching is denied, and his gracious promise of the Comforter to lead the disciples into "all the truth" is emptied of its meaning.

The same able writer in another place (p. 293) gives utterance to very remarkable views. After saying that we can now trace the degree in which the Master transcends the disciples, not the way they develop his teaching, but how they fail to do it, he proceeds: "Where Paul is greatest is where he is most directly under the influence or in the hands of Jesus, evolving the content of what he had received concerning him; where he is weakest is where his old scholasticism or his new antagonism dominates alike the form and substance of his thought. So with John: what in him is permanent and persuasive is of Christ; what is local and even trivial is of himself. To exhibit in full the falling off in the apostles cannot be attempted here; enough to say their conception of God is, if not lower, more outward, less intimate, or, as it were, from within; nor does it, with all its significance as to the absolute paternity, penetrate like a subtle yet genial spirit their whole mind, all their thought and all their being." The necessary result of such teachings is to create an impassable gulf between the gospels and the epistles, to darken the whole subject of inspiration, and to do grievous dishonor to the Holy Ghost. It takes a large part of the New Testament away from the rule of faith and subjects it to the judgment of the reader how far it represents the consciousness of Christ. It exaggerates the human element in the epistles so as to obscure and abridge the divine, and in fact leaves us with a mutilated standard of belief and practice.

It is, therefore, peculiarly appropriate to issue anew a work such as Mr. Bernard's, which is written without any tinge of a controversial spirit, and yet presents the common judgment of the church with clearness and accuracy. One might prefer that in analyzing the Pauline writings he had followed the chronological order, yet the author gives (pp. 166–7) satisfactory reasons for following the arrangement which occurs in the common English Bible, his object being not to show the relations of each one to the others, but rather their common characteristic as containing the fullness and maturity of Christian doctrine. He describes progress in its natural way as not a correction of what had gone before, but a further unfolding of the words and work of the blessed Master, and thus presents a complete statement of religious truth, in which every doctrine and precept finds its appropriate place, and ample materials are furnished for constructing a full-orbed and symmetrical system of theology and ethics.

TALBOT W. CHAMBERS.

NOV. 20, 1894.

EXTRACT

FROM

THE LAST WILL AND TESTAMENT

OF THE LATE

REV. JOHN BAMPTON,

CANON OF SALISBURY.

. . . "I give and bequeath my Lands and Estates to the Chancellor, Masters, and Scholars of the University of Oxford forever, to have and to hold all and singular the said Lands or Estates upon trust, and to the intents and purposes hereinafter mentioned; that is to say, I will and appoint that the Vice-Chancellor of the University of Oxford for the time being shall take and receive all the rents, issues, and profits thereof, and (after all taxes, reparations, and necessary deductions made) that he pay all the remainder to the endowment of Eight Divinity Lecture Sermons, to be established forever in the said University, and to be performed in the manner following:

"I direct and appoint, that, upon the first Tuesday in Easter Term, a Lecturer be yearly chosen by the Heads of Colleges only, and by no others, in the room adjoining to the Printing-House, between the hours of ten in the morning and two in the afternoon, to preach eight Divinity Lecture Sermons, the year following, at St. Mary's in Oxford, between the commencement of the last month in Lent Term, and the end of the third week in Act Term.

"Also I direct and appoint, that the eight Divinity Lecture Sermons shall be preached upon either of the following subjects —to confirm and establish the Christian Faith, and to confute all heretics and schismatics—upon the divine authority of the holy Scriptures—upon the authority of the writings of the primitive Fathers, as to the faith and practice of the primitive Church—upon the Divinity of our Lord and Saviour Jesus Christ—upon the Divinity of the Holy Ghost—upon the Articles of the Christian Faith, as comprehended in the Apostles' and Nicene Creeds.

"Also I direct, that thirty copies of the eight Divinity Lecture Sermons shall always be printed, within two months after they are preached; and one copy shall be given to the Chancellor of the University, and one copy to the Head of every College, and one copy to the Mayor of the city of Oxford, and one copy to be put into the Bodleian Library; and the expense of printing them shall be paid out of the revenue of the Land or Estates given for establishing the Divinity Lecture Sermons; and the preacher shall not be paid, nor be entitled to the revenue, before they are printed.

"Also I direct and appoint, that no person shall be qualified to preach the Divinity Lecture Sermons, unless he hath taken the degree of Master of Arts at least, in one of the two Universities of Oxford or Cambridge; and that the same person shall never preach the Divinity Lecture Sermons twice."

PREFACE.

THE title given to these Lectures may perhaps suggest different expectations as to their scope. It may appear to some to announce an intention of drawing from the New Testament materials for a historical inquiry into the growth of christian doctrine, as it took place in the minds and under the hands of the Apostles. To others it may indicate a purpose of showing that the New Testament itself exhibits a scheme of progressive doctrine, fashioned for permanent and universal use. The Lectures will be found to address themselves not to the first, but to the second of these attempts; not examining the New Testament collection in order to ascertain the chronological sequence of fact, but contemplating it, as it is, for the purpose of observing the actual sequence of thought. In so doing, we are concerned, not only with the component parts of the New Testament, but with the *order* in which they are placed. On this subject some prefatory words are needed, lest it should seem that the order here followed has been adopted *merely* because it comes naturally to *us*, as that with which we are familiar in our own Bibles.

When this particular arrangement of books, which may be, and often have been, otherwise arranged, is treated as involving a course of progressive teaching, it may seem that an unwarrantable stress is laid on an accidental order, which some may regard as little more than a habit of the printer and the binder. The

Lectures themselves ought to give the answer to this idea; for if the familiar order does exhibit a sequence of thought and a sustained advance of doctrine, then the several documents are in their right places, according to the highest kind of relation which they can bear to each other; and if they had come into our hands variously and promiscuously arranged, it would yet be incumbent on one who would study them as a whole, to place them before him in the same, or nearly the same, order as that which they have actually assumed.

It will be seen that the importance here ascribed to the order of the books is ascribed strongly to its chief divisions, and more faintly to its details. The four Gospels, the Book of Acts, the collection of Epistles, and the Apocalypse, are regarded as severally exhibiting definite stages in the course of divine teaching, which have a natural fitness to succeed each other. Within these several divisions, the order of the four Gospels is treated as having an evident doctrinal significance (Lecture II.), and a certain measure of propriety and fitness is attributed to the relative positions of the Pauline and the Catholic Epistles, and again in a less degree to that of the several Pauline Epistles themselves. (Lecture VI.)

But while it belongs to the scope of the Lectures to point out reasons of internal fitness for a certain arrangement of the books of the New Testament, it does not enter into their design to discuss the subject on its other side, and to treat of the custom of the Church in regard to the order of the canon. Yet this is a point on which, in some minds, inquiry will naturally arise, and to them some short account of the state of the case is due.

In speaking of the custom of the Church, it must first be remembered, that the New Testament was not given and received as one volume, but that it *grew together* by recognition and use. As the several books gradually coalesced into unity, it might be expected that there would be many varieties of arrangement, but that they would on the whole tend to assume their relative places, according to the law of internal fitness, rather than on any other principle which might exercise a transient influence, as, for instance, that of the relative dignity of the names of their authors, or that of their chronological production or recognition. In fact, this tendency shows itself at once, in the earliest period to which our inquiries are carried back by extant manuscripts, by catalogues of the sacred books given by ancient writers, and by the habitual arrangement of the oldest versions. A short summary of the testimony derived from these sources is given in the first Note in the Appendix, by reference to two writers whose works have laid the Church under no common obligations.(1) From that review of the case, it will be apparent that the order in which we now read the books of the New Testament is that which, on the whole, they have tended to assume; and that the general internal arrangement, by which the entire collection forms for us a consecutive course of teaching, has been sufficiently recognized by the instinct, and fixed by the habit, of the Church.

It remains to add a word of explanation as to the method in which the Progress of Doctrine in the New Testament has been here treated. Two ways of handling the subject may suggest themselves: one, that of exhibiting the gradual development of particular doctrines, through successive stages of the divine course of instruction; the other, that of marking the characteristics and functions of those stages themselves as parts of a progressive

(1) *Numbers within parentheses, in the text, refer to* NOTES *at the close of the volume; those without parentheses, to foot-notes.*

scheme. The first method would be suited to the purpose of *proving the fact* of the progress of doctrine; the second, to the purpose of *showing that that fact involves the unity of a divine plan*, and therefore the continuity of a divine authority. The latter purpose appeared the more likely to be practically useful, at least in the present day. The advanced character of the doctrine in some books, as compared with others, is indeed sufficiently obvious, and is not only admitted, but sometimes exaggerated into a supposed incongruity, or even inconsistency, in the views of the sacred writers. It was, then, not the reality of the progress of doctrine, but the true character of it, which seemed especially to solicit attention; and in this point of view the subject is here considered.

It was in fact originally suggested by the strong disposition, evinced by some eminent writers and preachers, to make a broad separation between the words of the Lord and the teaching of his Apostles, and to treat the definite statements of doctrine in the Epistles, rather as individual varieties of opinion on the revelation recorded in the Gospels, than as the form in which the Lord Jesus has perfected for us the one revelation of himself.

Such a habit of thought must frustrate the provision which our great Teacher has made for enduing those that believe on his name with the vigor of a distinct and the repose of a settled faith. One of the most effectual safeguards against that danger will be found in an intelligent appreciation of the progressive plan on which God has taught us in his written Word: and if the view which is taken in these Lectures of the range of New Testament teaching should, in any quarter and in any measure, contribute to that end, the prayer which has been associated with their preparation will have received its answer. In all our works the first and the last resort is the thought of that mercy which answers prayer. I have need to revert to it now. One who has taken up a subject connected with the Holy Word, under a strong sense of the usefulness which may belong to a due exposition of it, must feel a proportionate sorrow in the review of an inadequate treatment. But it is enough. The desires and the regrets which attend our ministrations in the Lord's household are better uttered to God than to man.

For one defect only it seems right to offer an excuse. I think that many of the points, which in the Lectures are necessarily touched in a cursory manner, ought to have been more fully worked out and illustrated in Notes and References; and it would certainly have been a satisfaction, in rapidly skirting the confines of so many fields of recent and laborious study, to borrow contributions from writers by whom they have been thoroughly explored. Only a few such additions have been made, as they occurred at the moment. I may be allowed to plead that the circumstances in which I was placed during the preparation of these Lectures have made it impossible for me to do more. Scarcely had this office been confided to me, before I was called to enter on the care of a parish of fifteen thousand souls, the affairs of which required immediate, and have compelled almost incessant attention. Of the effect of this pressure of duties it will not be proper for me to say more, than that it has caused the omission which is here acknowledged.

ANALYSIS OF THE LECTURES.

LECTURE I.

THE NEW TESTAMENT.

(*PAGE* 25.)

ST. JOHN xvii. 8.

SUBJECT proposed. Its connection with the ministry of the word, and with the present tendencies of thought.

I. PRELIMINARY POSITIONS.

1. There is *divine* teaching in the New Testament—doctrine given by the Father to the Son—by the Son to men.
2. The divine teaching *coincides in extent* with the New Testament. Not to be restricted to words of the Lord in the flesh. Effect of such restriction. Forbidden by the Lord's words. Not to be extended through the whole Christian age. Progress of doctrine through all Church history—is a progress of apprehension by man, not of communication by God. No advance in divine teaching after the apostolic age ever admitted by the Church.
3. The *plan* of the divine teaching is represented in the New Testament. In what sense it can be said that it exhibits a scheme of doctrine progressively developed.

II. OUTLINES OF THE SUBJECT.

1. *Reality* of the progress of doctrine. Visible in the Old Testament—in the New Testament.
2. *Stages* in the progress of doctrine in the New Testament—marked by Gospels, Acts, Epistles, Apocalypse.
3. *Principles* of the progress of doctrine in the New Testament—constituted by the relations of the doctrine (*a*) to its Author, (*b*) to the facts on which

LECTURE II.

THE GOSPELS.

ST. MARK i. 1.

LECTURE III.

THE GOSPELS.

HEB. iii. 3.

LECTURE IV.

THE ACTS OF THE APOSTLES.

ACTS i. 1-4.

testimony of the Apostles, to have involved the Gospel itself. Hence a divine authority attaches to the whole Apostolic teaching, in its interpretations and inferences as well as in its witness of facts.

II. THE METHOD IS CHANGED. Reason for the change. The change is a sign and means of progress. The history of salvation being finished, must be followed by the interpretation of it, and by the exhibition of its effects in human consciousness. This is achieved by the change in the method of divine teaching, signified by the words, "He dwelleth *with* you and shall be *in* you." Action of the indwelling Spirit to be distinguished according to its purpose — in the founders of the Church to communicate truth — in the members of the Church to receive it.

LECTURE V.

THE ACTS OF THE APOSTLES.

(*PAGE* 127.)

ACTS v. 42.

Further questions to be answered by the Book of Acts. Its purpose to answer them. Character and scheme of the Book. Its place and function in the evolution of doctrine.

I. IT GIVES THE GENERAL CHARACTER of the christian doctrine in its second stage.

1. A PREACHING OF CHRIST. Comparison of the preaching recorded in the Gospels and that recorded in the Acts — the one of the kingdom, the other of the person. The difference in the preaching accounts for the difference in the effect.

2. A PREACHING OF THE WORK OF CHRIST, in its main features and their results — of his death as the source of forgiveness, of his resurrection as the source of life. Progress of doctrine in the summing up and exposition of the past.

II. IT GIVES THE COURSE OF EVENTS through which the doctrine was matured. Outlines of the history in this point of view. The doctrine cleared and formed in the course of this history, chiefly in respect of two principles: *a. The Gospel is the substitute for the Law* — Jewish theory of the Law — Judaizing attempts negatived and superseded; *b. The Gospel is the new*

LECTURE VI.

THE EPISTLES.

Rom. i. 17.

THE

PROGRESS OF DOCTRINE

IN THE

NEW TESTAMENT

LECTURE I.

THE NEW TESTAMENT.

I HAVE GIVEN UNTO THEM THE WORDS WHICH THOU GAVEST ME.—
St. John xvii. 8.

ON the truth of this saying stands the whole fabric of creeds and doctrines. It is the ground of authority to the preacher, of assurance to the believer, of existence to the Church. It is the source from which the perpetual stream of Christian teaching flows. All our testimonies, instructions, exhortations, derive their first origin and continuous power from the fact that the Father has given to the Son, the Son has given to his servants, the words of truth and life.

I am now called, not so much to preach the words thus given to us, as to inquire concerning them. It is a secondary and subsidiary ministry.

Our first charge is, "Go stand and speak in the temple to the people all the words of this life." We go; and our words not only meet the wants of conscience, but stir the activities of thought; and a cloud of questions rises round us, which must be dissipated while it is gathering, but which will still gather while it is being dissipated. Thus the preaching of the words of life to the people is evermore attended by an incidental necessity for extensive and various discussion.

The institution of these lectures is a testimony to that necessity, and a testimony also to the relation which such discussion bears to the main object for which the Word was given. For if this pulpit is devoted on these occasions to the deliberate treatment of some particular question, that is only on account of the bearing which such questions may have on the work which the Church fulfils in testifying the Gospel of the grace of God. More especially is it fitting that one, who is habitually engaged in the work of preaching and teaching, should keep as near as he can to this ultimate practical aim. Therefore, invoking the guidance of God, I shall submit to you some considerations on the progress of doctrine in the New Testament, a subject which on the one side touches the living ministry of the Church at its very heart, and on the other is specially affected by the present tendencies of sacred criticism.

Into all our parishes and all our missions the thousands of evangelists, pastors, and teachers are sent forth with the Bible placed in their hands, and with solemn charges to draw from its pages the Gospel which they preach. But when those pages are opened, they present, not the exposition of a revelation completed, but the records of a revelation in progress. Its parts and features are seen, not as arranged after their development, but as arranging themselves in the course of their development, and growing, through stages which can be marked, and by accessions which can be measured, into the perfect form which they attain at last. Thus the Bible includes within itself a world of anticipation and retrospection, of preparation and completion, whereby various and vital relations are consti tuted between its several parts. These relations enter as really into the scheme of Scripture as do the several parts themselves; and must be rightly understood and duly appreciated, if the doctrine, which the Book yields upon the whole, is to be firmly grasped by the student or fairly presented by the preacher.

In this way the subject of progressive teaching in Scripture is implicated with the living ministry of the Church. How it is affected by the present tendencies of sacred criticism there is no need to explain, for it is known to all that the studies of our day are directed to a minute and laborious examination of the internal characteristics of the books of Scripture, and more particularly of their mutual relations, and of the differences of doctrine both in amount and form which they exhibit on comparison with each other. Notwithstanding all reasons for anxiety, sometimes even for grief and indignation, which we may find in the actual handling of the subject, we have cause to be thankful that the progressive character of revelation is thus coming more distinctly before the mind of the Church. In regard to any subject the observation of successive stages of design must be expected ultimately to conduce to a more thorough comprehension of the thing designed, and will also naturally tend to place the observer in closer contact with the mind of the designer. So will it be with the written word.

Only a part of the general subject is before us now. We shall be occupied with the last stage through which the revelation of God was perfected, as exhibited in the canonical books of the New Testament. But though only a part of a larger subject, this is itself one of great extent and various aspect, and on this account some preliminary words are necessary, in order to fix the point of view from which it will be regarded. I shall therefore devote the chief part of this introductory lecture to secure for myself the following positions.

1. That by doctrine shall be here meant *divine* teaching, or truth as communicated by God.

2. That the course of divine teaching under the Christian dispensation shall be considered to coincide in *extent* with the New Testament Scriptures.

3. That the relative character and actual order of the parts of the New Testament shall be taken, as adequately representing the progressive *plan* on which this course of divine teaching was perfected.

When I have strengthened these positions by such explanations as time will allow, I will close this introduction of the subject, by pointing out that the progressive system of teaching in the New Testament is an obvious *fact*, that it is marked by distinct *stages*, and that it is determined by natural *principles*.

I. 1. First, then, I assume that the doctrine here spoken of is *divine* teaching, and that by its progress is meant a systematic advance in its communication from God.

That *some* doctrine contained in the New Testament must be thus characterized, we are assured by the assertion of the Lord Jesus in the text: "I have given unto them the words which thou gavest me." Words then have been given to men, which, not only in their original source, but in their intermediate channel, are absolutely and incontestably divine. Over and above these discoveries of the mind of God which are contained in the natural order of things, and which we may discern by an intuitive faculty or infer by a reasoning process, we have that, which, in the clearest, fullest, strongest sense, must be called the "*word of God.*" Nay, he has not only given us *a word;* he has done more, he has given us *words*,[1] separate, articulate, definite communications, each as truly divine as is the whole word which they compose. Such words of God were spoken of in old time as "coming to" particular persons, who were to be the messengers of those words to others. The Prophets testified, when they spoke, that "the word of the Lord came to them;" and the testimony was authenticated of God and accepted of men. But the communications made through them were only introductory. "In sundry parts and in divers ways God having spoken of old to the Fathers in the Prophets, at the end of these days spake to us in his Son." Those to whom the word of God came were succeeded by him who is himself the "Word of God." He became man, and stood forth as the one real and eternal Prophet, the medium of communication between the mind of God and the mind of man. Then he was in the world, but he "was in heaven," in the concourse of men but "in the bosom of his Father." His flesh was as a veil between the two worlds, and he who dwelt in it read on the one side the secrets of the Most Holy, and on the other presented them to the apprehensions of mankind. On the one side he *received*, on the other he *gave*. He showed to the world the works which he had seen with his Father; he spoke to the world the words which he had heard with his Father; and in closing his personal teaching in the flesh, he lifted up his eyes to heaven and said, "I have given unto them the words which thou gavest me." Imagination itself can go no farther. If we asked for assurance that men had really

[1] ῥήματα,

received the words of God, it would be impossible to conceive a higher authority, a more plain assertion, or a more unqualified statement. On this point I need say no more. My only purpose in touching it has been to refresh in your minds the remembrance, that the doctrine about which we inquire is, in some part of it at least, truly and incontestably divine.

2. More perhaps needs to be said in order to justify the next step which I would take, in the assumption that the course of divine teaching *coincides in extent* with the Scriptures of the New Testament. Have I the right to extend the course of divine teaching so far? If so, have I the right to refuse to extend it farther? At first sight the text might suggest that the character of doctrine, which has been just asserted, should be limited to the words spoken by the lips of the Lord Jesus when on earth. If we pass beyond this, and include words spoken by the lips of men, we may seem compelled to extend our thoughts to a progress of doctrine carried on to the end of time. In neither of these cases will the course of the divine communication of Christian truth coincide with the extent of the New Testament. In the one case it will be comprised in the Gospels alone, which leave us some of their most peculiar doctrines only in short summaries or pregnant germs; in the other case it may be prolonged through an indefinite series of accessions, which will always leave the Church in doubt, as to what the faith delivered to it is, and still more in doubt as to what it may hereafter turn out to be.

What then are the words to which the description in the text applies? or rather, within what limits shall we seek them?

Undoubtedly the Lord speaks of all the words which he

had already uttered to those disciples as their teacher in the days of his flesh. But is the saying true *only* of those words? Is it to be restricted to that stage of teaching which had then reached its conclusion, and of which at the time the assertion might seem to be made? Or is it also true of other words? words for instance which he gave after he was risen? or, again, words which he gave after he was glorified?

To those who would study the evolution of doctrine in the New Testament this question is of vital importance, for if, after we have passed the first stage of teaching, the authority which we recognized there is withdrawn, our treatment of the subsequent teaching must be conducted in an altered spirit and on other principles. Having bowed in silence before the Divine Teacher, we shall recover our freedom of opinion when we are left with his followers. Only at first shall we tread securely on the rock: we must then look well to our steps, and be free to choose our path among the irregularities and uncertainties of a more shifting soil; for we shall pass from words which the Son of God gave to men, to the expansions of those words and the deductions from them which the men who first received them have given to us. Our study of the progress of doctrine within the limits of the New Testament would thus be entirely changed in its character, as we passed from the Gospels to the subsequent books. Only in the first stage would the progress of doctrine bear the meaning of the progress of its communication by God. In the second stage it could but signify the progress of its apprehension by men. The Acts and Epistles would thus form only the first chapter of the history of the Church, separated from its subsequent chapters by a much narrower interval than that which marks them off from the Gospels which precede them. They would in fact be simply *specimens* of human apprehensions of divine truth; specimens of singular value, because produced under peculiar advantages, but yet, like any other individual apprehensions, modified by the personal character and historical position of those who formed them. They would therefore be liable to such deductions on these accounts as historical criticism might suggest, and would remain rather as warrants for various explications by other minds and in other ages, than as fixed canons of the truth forever.

I ask, then, whether the giving of the words of God was completed when the text was uttered, or whether there was a distinct part of the process yet to come?

The discourse in which the saying occurs has supplied the answer. Its distinctive character is that of transition, closing the past but opening the future, representing a later stage of teaching as the predestined completion of the earlier, and cementing both into one, by asserting for both the same source, and diffusing over both the same authority. This function in the progress of divine teaching, which belongs to the discourse in the 14th, 15th, and 16th chapters of St. John, must come more distinctly into view at a later stage of our inquiry. It is now sufficient to refer to it in passing, as an evidence that the very words, of which the text specifically and indubitably speaks, include the assertion of the same divine gift and authority for other teaching which was yet to come.

Thus we stand on the declaration of the giver of the word himself, when we consider the progress of Christian doctrine in its communication from God as extending, not only over one stage in which it was delivered by the Lord in the flesh, but through a second stage in which it was delivered by the same Lord through the Spirit. It might indeed have seemed natural, at the point where the voice of Jesus ceases to draw the line which should terminate the words which were given by the Father to the Son, and by the Son were given to men, a line of broad demarcation, separating those words from all others whatever. But that very voice forbade the act, and admonished us that, when it should seem to have ceased, it must yet be recognized as carrying on the course of communications which were not then com plete. I now say no more on this important point, because a clear understanding upon it ought to be one of the chief results of the inquiry which lies before me.

But a second question is waiting for me now. If I see that the proposal to restrict the divine authority to the communications of the Lord's own lips has been negatived by himself, I am left to extend that authority to communications from the lips of men. Then where am I to stop? Am I any longer within the limits of the New Testament? I have looked forth on the ocean. Am I, or am I not, actually launched upon it? I am compelled to turn towards the vast and confusing prospect, in order to mark the limits within which I claim the right to remain.

Now if the second part of the New Testament simply rehearsed to us certain definite revelations, which the writers alleged that they had received, no difficulty would exist. Their testimony to these would be on the same footing (or nearly so) with the testimony of the Evangelists as to the discourses of our Lord. But this is not their method. We have the revealed truth presented to us in the Epistles, not only as a communication from God, but also as an apprehension by man. The great transition from the one stage to the other is exhibited before our eyes as already effected. We have the gospel as it existed in the mind of Peter and of Paul, of James and of John. It is thus presented to us in combination with the processes of human thought and the variations of human feelings, in association with peculiarities of individual character, and in the course of its more perfect elaboration through the exigencies of events and controversies.

But is not this account of the second part of the New Testament also the account of the whole subsequent history of doctrine in the world, that is, of Church history, in its essential and inward character? Certainly it is so; and therefore the Acts and the Epistles stand to the ecclesiastical historian as the first chapters of his work, for there he already finds the aspects which the revealed truth bears to human minds and assumes in human hands, and the manner in which its parts and proportions come to be distinctly exhibited through the agency of men and the instrumentality of facts. And this is a process which goes on through descending ages, and in which every generation bears its part. It has gained accessions from all those varieties of the human mind which have been placed in contact with revealed truth, from the idiosyncracies of persons, of nations, of ages, from Fathers and Councils, from controversies and heresies, from Hellenist, Alexandrian, and Roman forms of thought, from the mind of the East and the mind of the West, from corruptions and reformations of religion, from Italy and England, from Germany and Geneva, from authority and inquiry, from Church and Dissent. These words and others like them represent the varying measures of apprehension, and the varying kinds of expression, which the Gospel revelation has found among men. The "Developments of doctrine" (to use a word which some time since was very familiar to many of us) — the developments of doctrine thus originated were the joint product of the revealed truth and the condition of the mind which received it. The revealed truth was one, but the conditions of the human mind are infinitely various, and hence an endless variety in the developments themselves, — a variety which sometimes melts into a higher harmony, but more often jars on our ears in irreconcilable discord.

I am not here concerned with the degrees in which different developments have represented or perverted truth, and in which they have more conspicuously exhibited the element of the divine truth or that of the human infirmity. I would only observe that through all this confusion there is in some sense a progress of doctrine. Even by misapprehensions and perversions the relations of the Word to the human mind are more perfectly disclosed. In partial systems of religion those parts of the entire scheme which they have more particularly adopted often come to be seen under a stronger light. But especially it is evident that certain great features of truth emerge from periods of conflict and the driving mists of controversy, and swell upon the sight with outlines more defined and a power more recognized than had seemed to belong to them before. The names of Athanasius, Augustine, and Luther, recall in a moment some of the most obvious examples of this fact, in regard to the doctrines of the Nature of Christ, of Original Sin, and of Justification by Faith.

There were periods then at which these doctrines stood forth with a vividness, precision, and force, which gave them as it were a new place in the apprehensions of men, affecting of course by their increased definiteness and expansion the proportions of the whole body of truth. These however are only prominent instances of a general and continuous fact. Every age, every Church, every sect, every controversy, in some way or other contributes something to the working out, the testing, or the illustrating of some part of the revelation of God. Our English mind has borne its part, and the religious movements of our own day will deposit some residuum of materials for future thought and knowledge. Our missionary efforts will, in this respect also, have results of their own, and Christianity in India or in China, when it has in some degree lost its English type, and entered into full relations with the peculiar minds of those peculiar races, will perhaps make as distinct additions to the history of doctrine, as we recognize in passing from the theology of the Eastern to that of the Western Church. The history upon the whole both has been and will be a long disclosure of the perverse tendencies and infirm capacities of man. Yet a special providence over the Church and the Living Spirit in it has been proved as well as promised: and he who looks back upon the tortuous and agitated course of thought, perceives that the truth is not only preserved, but in some sense advanced, the definitions of it becoming more exact, the construction of it more systematic, and the deductions from it more numerous.

Thus the history of the apprehension of Christian truth by man, which commences within the New Testament, is continued in the history of the Church to the end of time; and still, while it is continued, it is in some sort a history of progress, and one in which the Spirit of God mingles, and which the providence of God moulds.

What then is it which draws the line of separation between the apostolic period and all the subsequent periods of this history? It is this — That the apostolic period is *not only* a part of the history *of the apprehension of truth by man:* it is *also* a part of the history of *the communication of truth by God.* It is the first stage of the one, and the last stage of the other. The aspect which the Gospel bears in the writings of the Apostles is a communication from God of what it really is, a revelation of what he intended that it should be in the minds of men forever. This character of the apostolic writings has, without variation of testimony, been acknowledged by the Church from the beginning; but this acknowledgment has been *confined* to these writings, and has never been extended to subsequent expositions or decrees. Councils and doctors have claimed a right to be heard, only as asserters and witnesses of apostolic teaching. No later communications from heaven are supposed or alleged. What has been handed down, — what is collected out of the writings of the Apostles — is the professed authority for all definitions and decrees; and all reference to (what may appear to be) other authority is based upon the fact, asserted or implied, that in the quarters appealed to there was reason to recognize some special connection with the apostolic teaching. This fact, moreover, comes out most clearly at those moments in which (what might be called) an advance of doctrine is seen most evidently to take place. If the doctrine of the Nature of Christ shows a new distinctness and firmness of outline after Nice and Constantinople, yet that form of the doctrine professes to be, and when examined proves to be, only a formal definition of the original truth. Nothing new has been imported into it; only fresh verbal barriers have excluded importations which were really new. If the doctrine of Justification by Faith seems, at the era of the

Reformation, like a new apparition on the scene, yet it is advanced, and is received, only as the old Pauline doctrine reasserting its forgotten claims.

Even palpable innovations have supported their pretensions by the plea of an imaginary tradition, descending from the days when it was confessed that the communications of God had been completed. Our own days have seen fresh evidence of the tenacity with which the Romish Church holds to this theory, while making that last addition to the articles of the faith which seemed to imply that it was abandoned. Then, when the pretence of a tradition appeared to have finally given way under the ever accumulating mass of novelties, minds accustomed to the logic of facts began to cast about for some other theory, which should admit of being reconciled with them. The exposition of such a theory began in this pulpit, and was completed in the communion into which its author speedily passed. It was a theory which virtually claimed for the Church the power to create new doctrine, instead of a mere authority to determine what was old. But the claim could not secure adoption, though it had been boldly acted upon, and seemed necessary to the controversial position of Rome. The settled sense of Christendom as to the revelation of the truth was not to be violated. Newly-"*defined*" doctrines were still to be pronounced true and necessary on the ground that they had been held by the Apostles, though no evidence of that fact survived, and that they had been handed down by tradition, though no trace of the tradition could be found. The gift thus ascribed to the "Infallible Authority" was not an inspiration to know the truth of new doctrines, but a revelation of the fact that they were old. The new position has been in fact abandoned by those who offered, but have not been suffered to hold it [2]; and we are still able to say, that only in transient moments of enthusiasm, and by some insignificant and eccentric sects, has there been any definite allegation, that doctrinal communications from God have been received since the last Apostle died.

The sum of what has been said is this. (First), There are words (definite doctrinal communications) of which it is said by the Lord Jesus, "The words which thou gavest me I have given them." (Secondly), These words are not only those which he spake with his lips in the days of his flesh; they include other words, afterwards given through men in the Spirit, during a period of time which is represented to us by the books of the New Testament. (Thirdly), Those words were finished in that period, and have received no subsequent additions. The description in the text not only cannot be shown to belong, but has never been supposed to belong, to any words which have been spoken since.

On these three points the judgment of the Church has been all but universal and unchanging. In speaking therefore of progress of doctrine in the New Testament, I speak of a course of communication from God which reaches its completion within those limits, constituting a perfected scheme of divine teaching, open to new elucidations and deductions, but not to the addition of new materials.

3. The books of the New Testament are the form into which this divine teaching has been thrown for permanent and universal purposes, and by the will of God they constitute the only representation of it for all men and for ever. I have now to add that they give the representation,

not only of its substance, but also of the *plan* on which it was progressively matured.

It must here be remarked that there are two ways in which we may exhibit the progressive development of any system of things, whether it be a scheme of religious doctrine, a science, a political constitution, or anything else which has completed itself by degrees — one of which may be characterized as the *historical*, the other as the *constructive* method. In the one case we inquire after the exact succession of events through which the result was reached; in the other we discriminate the stages of advance in the result itself. The representation of progress made in the one case would be regulated simply by the order of fact, while that which would be produced in the other would be rather governed by the order of thought. Now if we consider the New Testament as representing a progressive development of doctrine, it is so in the latter sense more than in the former. It is rather a constructive than a simply historical representation. For instance, in the development of the manifestation of Christ in the flesh, the words and deeds recorded by St. John must be restored, on the historic principle, to their proper places in the actual order of events; on the constructive principle, they properly coalesce into a separate whole, as bringing out a view of that manifestation, which is an advance in the order of thought upon the view which the synoptic Gospels present. So in a historic representation of the formation of apostolical doctrine we should have to trace the successive steps and occasions of its advance, to secure the exact chronological arrangement of St. Paul's Epistles, and to insert them in their several places in the narrative of his labors. On the other hand, the purposes of a constructive representation may be better served by keeping the records of the external activity of the Church separate from its directly doctrinal writings, or by placing those doctrinal writings in a different order from that of their chronological production. Thus the New Testament, as a whole, presents to us a course of teaching on the constructive rather than on the historic principle; and it is in this sense that I propose to take the book as an adequate representation, not only of the substance of the divine teaching, but of the plan and order of its progress.

It may be said, that there is a difference between the progress of doctrine as it actually was during the time which the New Testament covers, and the representation of it which we have in those particular writings. Yes! and there would be a difference between the actual course of some important enterprise, — say of a military campaign for instance, — and the abbreviated narrative, the selected documents, and the well-considered arrangement, by which its conductor might make the plan and execution of it clear to others. In such a case the man who read would have a more perfect understanding of the mind of the actor and the author than the man who saw; he would have the whole course of things mapped out for him on the true principles of order. Such is the position of every reader of the New Testament, who accounts that the Lord, by whom the historical development of truth was guided, is also the virtual author of that representation of it which lies before him.

We have not, then, to make out a chart from materials given to us, but to study one which is already made. Tracing the course of doctrine as it is seen to advance through those pages, we shall have no need to reconstruct for ourselves the actual order in which the truth was historically developed. Whatever were the measures and gradations by which it was opened out to the Church at first, here are the measures and gradations by which it is opened out to the Church forever. Indeed, the plan on which the Lord perfected his promised teaching was one which *could* only be seen in retrospect. Conducted through the medium of persons and events, and by the use of local occasions, the method of procedure must at the time have very imperfectly disclosed its real system and coherence. Parts of the truth, for instance, were being cleared and settled in some Churches, which perhaps were scarcely inquired for in others, yet the decision was of the Lord, and destined for the whole body. A transient occasion demanded the interference of a particular Apostle, and through his sentence was given some fundamental and eternal principle. Among all that was done and written and said, in that scene of intense activity and incessant movement which the apostolic writings open to us, it would have been hard indeed at the time to follow with steady eye the great lines of advancing doctrine, and to single out the acts and documents which would adequately represent the results secured. Only when these results had been firmly deposited in the Church, could the successive contributions of the divine teaching be recognized, and their relative order discerned. To exhibit this plan of things there was need, not of a mass of accidental records, but of a body of records selected and arranged. It might seem that we had no right to attribute such a character as this to a collection of writings which are upon the face of them independent and occasional. Yet it is certain that, when taken as a whole, this is its *effect*, and that it makes upon the mind the impression of unity and design. He who reads through the Koran (albeit the work of a single author) finds himself oppressed, as by a shapeless mass of accidental accretions. He who reads through the New Testament finds himself educated as by an orderly scheme of advancing doctrine. The several books seem to have grown into their places as component parts of an organic whole; and "the New Testament of our Lord and Saviour Jesus Christ" lies before us as an account of a perfected revelation, and a course of divine teaching designed and prepared by one presiding mind.

II. Having now accomplished the preliminary steps, I will close this introductory Lecture by pointing out the *reality* of the progress of which I speak, the *stages* through which it is perfected, and the *principles* by which it is regulated.

1. The *reality* of this progress is very visible; and more especially so when we regard the New Testament as the last stage of that progressive teaching which is carried on through the Scriptures as a whole. Glance from the first words to the last, "In the beginning God created the heavens and the earth" — "Even so, come, Lord Jesus." How much lies between these two! The one the first rudiment of revelation addressed to the earliest and simplest consciousness of man, that, namely, which comes to him through his senses, the consciousness of the material world which lies in its grandeur round him: the other the last cry from within, the voice of the heart of man, such as the intervening teaching has made it; the expression of the definite faith which has been found, and of the certain hope which has been left by the whole revelation of God. The course of teaching which carries us from the one to the other is progressive throughout, but with different rates of progress in the two stages which divide it. In the Old Testament the progress is protracted, interrupted, often languid, some-

times so dubious as to seem like retrogression. Accessions take place in sundry parts, in divers manners, at times under disguises of earthly forms, seeming to suggest mistakes, which have to be themselves corrected. Yet through it all the doctrine grows, and the revelation draws nearer to the great disclosure. Then there is entire suspension. We turn the vacant page which represents the silence of 400 years, — and we are in the New Testament.

Now again there is progress, but rapid and unbroken. Our steps before were centuries; now they are but years. From the manger of Bethlehem on earth to the city of God coming down from heaven the great scheme of things unrolls before us, without a check, without a break. It is in harmony with processes of nature and with human feelings, that preparations should be slowly matured, but that final results should rapidly unfold. When life becomes intense it can no more endure delays, or develop itself by languid progression. The root was long before it showed the token of its presence, the stem and leaves grew slowly, but yesterday the bud emerged from its sheath, and to-day it is expanded in the flower. A swift course of events, the period of one human life, a few contemporary writers have given us all the gospel that we need to know under our present dispensation, all that we shall ever know till Jesus comes again.

But there is, as has been observed, a plan of progress though its course is swift, and I would take note first of its stages and then of its principles.

2. Its *stages* I do not now examine; but just mark them off as they catch the eye. First we are conducted through the manifestation of Christ in the flesh: we see and hear and learn to know the li ing person, who is at once the

source and the subject of all the doctrine of which we speak. He is presented as the *source* of doctrine, delivering with his own lips the first Christian instructions, the first preaching of a present gospel and the pregnant principles of truth. He is presented as the *subject* of doctrine, for it is himself that he offers to us by word and deed as the object of our faith, and the events which we see accomplished in his earthly history are the predestined substance of all subsequent instruction. But within this stage of learning there is not only continuous development by the course of events and accumulation of facts, but at a certain point a great change occurs, which is visible to every eye. It is the point where we pass from the synoptic Gospels and come under the teaching of St. John. Now we rise to heaven, and go back to "the beginning," and set forth from "the bosom of the Father." Now we are taught to recognize the glory of the person of Christ, with a consciousness not changed but more distinct, with acknowledgments not new but more articulate. In the former Gospels we have walked with him in the common paths of life; in this we seem to have joined him on "the holy mount." It is almost like the change which was witnessed by the three disciples, who had walked conversing by his side, and then suddenly saw his countenance altered and his raiment white and glistering. Such is the effect upon our minds, not merely of the last Evangelist's own expressions, but of that selection of words and acts which it was his commission to make and to leave.

We close the Gospels and open the books which follow We have passed a great landmark and are farther on our way; yet the line of doctrine which we pursue seems to have sunk to a lower level, for we cease to be taught by the lips of the Incarnate Word, and are remitted to the discourses and writings of men. Is this progress? He assured us that it would be; and we find that it is.

We are under the dispensation of the Spirit; and in the book of Acts are borne, by seeming accident but by invisible guidance, straight along that line of fact and of thought in which we are to find the full developments of the truth which was given in the Gospels.

In matter of doctrine the book of Acts is our introduction to the Epistles. Here if the authority of the teacher seems lowered from what it was in the Gospels, the fulness of the doctrine is visibly increased. Its more mysterious parts are seen expanded and defined. Statements which might seem of doubtful meaning in the former stage have found a fixed interpretation in the latter. Suggestions of thought in the one have become habits of thought in the other. What were only facts there have become doctrines here; and truths, which just gleamed from a parable, or startled us in some sudden saying, are now deliberately expanded into manifold and recognized relations with the feelings and necessities of man. The nature and consequences of the work of Christ on earth, the offices for men which he now fulfils in heaven, the living relations which he bears to his people in the Spirit, the discoveries of his majesty and communication of his glory which are ready to be revealed in the last time, all these are seen in the apostolic writings, sometimes asserted as perspicuous doctrine, more often blending and kindling together in the inward life of the Spirit, giving the form to the character and the motives to the life.

Yet a further change takes place as we reach the close of the Scriptures. This inward and personal life in the Spirit is not all. There is a kingdom of Christ, which has its form, its history, its destinies. In the later Epistles we see a constituted society, and hear the sounds of a coming conflict: the Church appears on the defensive, and the steps of invisible powers are moving round her. The prophetic book which follows transports us into the unseen world, and opens the temple of God in heaven, and shows us the connection of the history of the Church with things above and things below; and guides through the dim confusion of the conflict to the last victory of the Lamb, leaving us at last among the full effects of redemption, in a new heaven and a new earth, and in a holy society and city of God.

3. Having cast our eye along the stages of advance, we next inquire after the *principles* by which it is governed; and we find them in the relations which the doctrine bears to its author, which it bears to the facts on which it is founded, which it bears to the human mind to which it is addressed, and which its component parts bear to each other.

a. The relation of the doctrine to its *author* is the ground of its continuous unity, and unless there be unity we have no right to speak of progress: for succession is of many, but progress is of one. The unity of the New Testament doctrine lies in this, that it is the teaching of *one* mind, the mind of Christ. The security for this is given to us in two ways: first by the fact that there is no part of the later and larger doctrine which has not its germs and principles in the words which he spake with his own lips in the days of his flesh. It is provided that all which is to be spoken after shall find support and proof from his own pregnant and forecasting sayings. Secondly, it is made clear by his own promises beforehand, by facts which evidence his personal administration, and by the distinct assertions of the men whom he employs, that, when his own voice has ceased on earth, it is nevertheless he who teaches still. The testimonies of this are scattered along our whole path, till we come to the last vision itself, in which he personally reappears, "to show unto his servants the Revelation which God gave unto him," renewing thereby for the last time the assertion of our text, "I have given unto them the words which thou gavest me."

b. The relation of the doctrine to the *facts* on which it is founded is a principle by which a certain measure of progress is necessarily constituted. Christian doctrine does not ground itself on speculation. It begins from the region and the testimony of the senses. Its materials are facts, and it is itself the interpretation and application of them. It is therefore reasonable that the facts should be completed, before they are clearly interpreted and fully applied. Jesus must have died and risen again before the doctrine concerning his death and resurrection can be brought to light. Not till the Son of Man is glorified can we expect to arrive at a stage of doctrine which shall give all the meaning and the virtue of facts which till then were not completed. Up to that time we are in the midst of a history of which his own saying is true, "What I do thou knowest not now, but thou shalt know hereafter."

c. The relation of the doctrine to the *human mind* does also plainly necessitate a particular kind of progress in the method of its communication. The doctrine was not meant to be an opinion but a power: "The words that I speak unto you, they are spirit and they are life." It therefore had to pass from the form of a divine announcement into the form of a human experience. It had to establish its own connection with the world of human thoughts and feelings. Once spoken by the mouth of the Lord, it might perhaps have been left to make this transition according to the natural laws of the human mind. But the transition in itself was too great, the consequences of error in the first stage of it would be too momentous, for the Author and Finisher of our faith to leave the Church to her ordinary resources at so critical a moment. He would give a divine certainty and authority to the first human apprehensions of his truth. He would make it sure that he had himself conducted those first experiences and applications of the word, by which future experiences and applications might be guided and tried forever. Therefore the word spoken *to* men by the voice of Jesus changed into a word spoken *in* men by his Spirit, creating thus a kind of teaching which carried his word into more intimate connection with human thought and more varied application to human life.

d. Lastly, the relation of the *several parts* of doctrine to each other would call for a certain orderly course of development. There is a natural fitness that the knowledge of the Lord himself should precede the knowledge of his work, and that we should wait on his ministry on earth before we apprehend his ministry in heaven, and that we should see that we are reconciled by his death before we understand how we are saved by his life; embracing the meritorious means before we expatiate among the glorious issues. It is reasonable that an acquaintance with Christ himself, and a knowledge of his work and grace, should be given first, and that, from the source thus provided, the rules and motives of conduct should afterwards be elicited. It is right that we should be fully and clearly instructed in the things of our present dispensation, and in the life of faith through which we are passing now and in the kingdom of an inward and spiritual grace, and then that we should be subsequently informed, and more dimly and briefly too, of the great history of the unseen conflict with which we are more remotely concerned, and of its final issues when the former things will have passed away and God shall make all things new. These various parts of the doctrine, though in some degree commingling and interfused, do yet on the whole sort themselves out in Gospels, Epistles, and Apocalypse

Lift up now your eyes on this monument of a distant age which you call the New Testament. Behold these remains of the original literature of a busy Jewish sect; these occasional writings of its leaders, emanating from different hands and gathered from different localities. They are delivered to you collected and arranged, though by means which you cannot ascertain. They are before you now, not as accidentally collected writings, but as one book; a design completed, a body organized, and pervaded by one inward life The several parts grow out of and into each other with mutual support, correlative functions, and an orderly development. It is a "whole body fitly joined together and compacted by that which every joint supplies, according to the effectual working in the measure of every part, making increase of the body to the building itself up" in truth.

It begins with the person of Christ, and the facts of his manifestation in the flesh, and the words which he gave from his Father; and accustoms us by degrees to behold his glory, and to discern the drift of his teaching and to expect the consequences of his work. It passes on to his body the Church, and opens the dispensation of his Spirit, and carries us into the life of his people, yea down into the secret places of their hearts; and there translates the announcements of God into the experiences of man, and discovers a conversation in heaven and a life which is hid with Christ in God. It works out practical applications, and is careful in the details of duty, and provides for difficulties and perplexities, and suggests the order of Churches, and throws up barriers against the wiles of the devil. It shows us things to come, the course of the spiritual conflict, and the close of this transient scene, and the coming of the Lord, and the resurrection of the dead, and the eternal judgment, and the new creation, and the life everlasting.

Thus it is furnished for all emergencies and prepared for perpetual use. It dominates the restless course of thought, and is ever being interpreted by experience and events. It is an authority which survives when others perish, and a light which waxes when others wane. By it, as the instrument of God for the education of men, nations are humanized and churches sanctified. And yet more real and lasting than these are the ultimate results which it secures. An elect nation is being gathered from among us, and an eternal Church prepared, which shall supplant all transient and provisional societies in that day for which the whole creation waits. Here is the final scope of the Book of our covenant, in its combination with that older volume which it continues and completes.

Then is it not to each of us a matter of the deepest personal concern, that the truth which it teaches and the spirit which it breathes should have entered into his own soul; and that he should thus become a partaker in the life which it reveals, an example of the character which it demands, and an inheritor of the portion which it promises? But this cannot be, unless he yield to the Written Word the *confidence* which it claims. Oh! deal worthily, deal trustfully with such a guide as this! Venture your souls on the words of which the Lord has said, "I have given unto them the words which thou gavest me." Receive the message, receive the form in which it is left to you, "not as the word of man, but as it is in truth, the word of God," and then you will find that it "effectually worketh also in them that believe"; for he who "obeys from the heart that form of doctrine into which he is delivered," finds that a course of progressive teaching is opened in his own soul, to which the Holy Scripture will never cease to minister, and which the Holy Spirit will never cease to guide.

LECTURE II.

THE GOSPELS.

THE BEGINNING OF THE GOSPEL OF JESUS CHRIST, THE SON OF GOD.
St. Mark i. 1.

WITH reverential and affectionate interest we look back to the beginnings of those things which possess our allegiance as established powers, or are daily enjoyed as familiar blessings. The thought that they had a beginning, that there was once a time when they were not, gives a freshness to the feelings with which we regard them; while the comparison of the state of commencement with the state of perfection brings with it a natural pleasure, in marking the tendencies and the tokens of all that has happened since. No words can open the heart to these impressions so powerfully as those which have just been uttered. The beginning of the Gospel of Jesus Christ, the Son of God, places us at the opening of the mystery of godliness, of the salvation of the world, of the glory which fills the heavens, and of the kingdom which endures forever.

The expression with which St. Mark opens his narrative implies that the Gospel is then an established fact and a completed scheme, and that he here returns to the moment when the fact began to assert itself before the world as already present, and the scheme to show itself as in actual progress. The beginning of the Gospel (according to this Evangelist) is not found at the birth of Jesus, when the communications of Heaven were made but to few, and died suddenly into silence; but from the time when John did baptize in the wilderness, and when Jesus began to show himself, and "the word of the beginning of Christ" was publicly proclaimed, never to be again suspended till it should have become the word of a completed Gospel. It is indeed the habit of the Apostles to represent the publication of the Gospel as historically commencing at the same point of time. "The word," says St. Peter, "which God sent unto the children of Israel, preaching peace by Jesus Christ, — that word began from Galilee, after the baptism which John preached;[1] and St. Paul, in presenting to the Jews "the word of this salvation," dates its proclamation from the time "when John had first preached before his coming the baptism of repentance to all the people of Israel."[2]

But the expression which is used in the text of the opening of the public life of Jesus may also be truly applied to the whole period of that life. The Gospel, considered as *fact*, began from the Incarnation, and was completed at the Resurrection; but the Gospel, considered as *doctrine*, began from the first preaching of Jesus, and was completed in the dispensation of the Spirit. When the Lord quitted the world, he left the material of the Gospel already perfect, but the exposition of the Gospel only begun; and in the subsequent consciousness of his disciples, the period of the commencement of the word and the period of its perfection must have been strongly discriminated from each other.

When living in the perfect dispensation of the Spirit, and going to others in the fulness of the blessing of the

[1] Acts x. 36, 37. [2] Ibid. xii 24.

Gospel of Christ, they would remember how that Gospel dawned gradually on their minds during the few years in which its facts had been passing before their eyes, how imperfectly they had understood those facts, how inadequately they had apprehended the teaching by which the facts were accompanied, how true it was that what their Lord did they knew not then, but that they were to know it afterwards. To them that whole period of time must have seemed but an initiatory stage, a "*beginning* of the Gospel of Jesus Christ the Son of God."

And so it was. The Gospel which Jesus preached was a Gospel which in its main particulars had yet to be fulfilled, and which could not be fully opened till it had been fulfilled. While the facts were still incomplete, the doctrine was yet in its commencement; and we have on this account the right to describe by the words of the text, not only the *first steps* but the *whole* of the manifestation of Christ in the flesh. The beginning of the Gospel is a name which in one sense comprehends "all that Jesus *began* both to do and teach until the day when he was taken up."

To us this stage of the divine teaching is represented by the writings of the four Evangelists; and I would now consider this collection, first *relatively*, as the beginning of the orderly development of the Christian doctrine in the whole New Testament, and then *separately*, as a course of teaching which bears within its own limits a certain character of systematic advance.

Two such topics, included in a single Lecture, can receive little more than a suggestive treatment; but I pray that this may not occasion any defect of that careful reverence with which the fourfold Gospel must be ever touched by those who see in it the very ark of the covenant, where the cherubim of glory overshadow the mercy-seat.

I. First, then, we have to observe how the Gospel collection *is fitted to its place and fulfils its function, as the commencement of the Christian doctrine in the New Testament.*

Now the Christian doctrine is a doctrine concerning *facts* which have occurred and *a person* who has been manifested within the sphere of human observation. The foundations of all that is to be known of the word of life are laid in "that which was seen with the eyes, and heard with the ears, and handled with the hands" of men. Then it is necessary for every learner that, before all inferences or applications, the facts themselves as mere phenomena should first be rendered in the clearest light. Hence our elementary lessons are narratives of the simplest form. A plain report of words and deeds, easy and inartificial in the extreme, in which the most stupendous events elicit no articulate expression of feeling, without appearance of plan or system, with scarcely a comment or reflection, and in which a word of explanation almost startles us — such is the character of the three first of those writings which form the ground and contain the material of all subsequent Christian doctrine. No literary fact is more remarkable than that men, knowing what these writers knew, and feeling what they felt, should have given us chronicles so plain and calm. They have nothing to say as from themselves. Their narratives place us without preface, and keep us without comment, among external scenes, in full view of facts, and in contact with the living person whom they teach us to know. The style of simple recital, unclouded and scarcely colored by any perceptible contribution from the mind of the writers, gives us the scenes, the facts, and the person, as seen in the clearest light and through the most transparent atmosphere. Who can fail to recognize a divine provision for placing the disciples of all future ages as nearly as possible in the position of those who had been personally present at "the beginning of the Gospel of Jesus Christ the Son of God?"

The importance, in the whole course of instruction, of first fixing on the mind both the objective reality of the facts and the living portrait of the person, is further intimated by the *fourfold* repetition of the history. Four times does the Lord walk before us in the glory of grace and truth, and, whatever correspondences or variations the Gospels may exhibit in other parts of their narratives, four times are the great facts of the death and resurrection of Christ rehearsed to us in the minuteness of circumstantial detail. We do not go forward to further disclosures, till the historical facts have been insured to us by testimony upon testimony, and the portrait has grown familiar to us by line upon line.

Far on in the holy books, when the scriptural structure is nearly perfected, our eyes are turned back to the ground of visible, audible, tangible realities from which we started.

"That which was from the beginning, which we have heard, which we have seen with our eyes, which we have looked upon, and our hands have handled of the Word of life (for the life was manifested, and we have seen it, and bear witness, and show unto you that eternal life, which was with the Father and was manifested to us), that which we have seen and heard declare we unto you, that ye also may have fellowship with us."[1]

Yes, it is true. We *have* fellowship with those that

[1] 1 John i. 1-3.

speak, not only in their spiritual relations with their Lord (which they fully understood only after he was gone), but in their remembrances of him in that earlier time when he was yet with them. Their witness is effectual for this end. For *us* also it is all real. He dwelt among us. We beheld his glory. We caught the gracious words that proceeded out of his mouth. So things went with him. So he looked and moved and spoke. So he wrought and suffered and died. We have stood by the cross of Jesus. We have entered the empty sepulchre. We have seen him alive after his passion. He has shown us his hands and his feet. We have been led out as far as to Bethany, have seen the hands lifted up to bless, and watched the ascending form.

Open these pages where we will, the sense of reality revives within us. We feel afresh that we have not followed cunningly devised fables, have not loved an idea, or trusted in an abstraction. We know in whom we have believed, and feel that our Redeemer is our friend. We are solemnized as in a holy sanctuary, and secure as in a familiar home. We have escaped from doubt and debate, and no longer criticise or reason. We have recovered the mind of little children. We sit at the feet of Jesus: and the faith which came into his presence languid and disconcerted, departs invigorated and refreshed.

Brethren, let me urge upon you the habitual study of the holy Gospels for this revival of the reality and simplicity of faith. Let me urge it more especially upon those who converse in the region of abstract ideas, whether they frequent the ordered paths of systematic divinity, or wander in the free excursions of speculative thought. Dear as the Gospel stories are to the simple peasant, they are yet more necessary to the student and the divine; for there are influences in abstract thought and in dogmatic discussion which will drain the soul of life unless fitting antidotes be used: and there is no antidote so effectual, as is found in a continual return to those scenes of historic fact in which the word of God has given us our first lessons in Christ.

This necessity for habitual converse with the evangelical narratives is a sufficient proof of the wisdom which assigned them the place and the space which they actually fill, and especially which ordained that the picture of our Lord's earthly life should be given to us not in one Gospel, but in four.

I suppose we all feel how different would have been the effect of possessing one "Life of Christ," however full and systematic. We spend more time, and (if I may use the expression) feel more at home, in the four successive chambers than we should have done in one long gallery; and the impression of all that is there shown to us sinks deeper into the heart, from the repetition of many passages of the story under slightly varying lights and in different relative connections. Lively attention, minute observation, careful comparison, and inquiry which is never fully satisfied, are awakened at every step by that singular combination of resemblances and differences; and the mind is thus engaged to dwell longer on the scenes, conversing among them in a more animated spirit, and with an interest which is perpetually refreshed. We know the immense expenditure of labor in our own day on the comparative characteristics of the Gospels, and the manifold attempts to harmonize or to reconstruct them, to ascertain the point of view of the writers, and to account for the variations in their selection and position of incidents and in the turn which they give to discourses. Whatever be the spirit in which such attempts are made, they at least afford an incidental witness to the care which divine wisdom has taken to detain and occupy our minds at the outset in those scenes in which alone we can learn to know Jesus Christ *himself.*

It is plain that the four histories are modified by their own instinctive principles of selection and arrangement, which do not indeed announce themselves, and almost elude our attempts to ascertain them, but yet result in giving four discriminated aspects of their common subject, as the Royal Lawgiver, the Mighty Worker, the Friend of Man, and the Son of God — four aspects, but one portrait; for if the attitude and the accessories vary, the features and the expression are the same. (3)

Who does not perceive the immense assistance hereby given to us for receiving the knowledge of Christ? One representation, however full, would still have suggested the thought, "This is the impression made upon a single mind. Who can say what part of it is due to the idiosyncrasies of the witness? If we had the impressions of another mind, perhaps we should have a different image." As it is, we derive the impression from four different quarters, and the image is still the same. It is represented from four different points of view; but, however represented, it is the same Jesus. The conception is one, and its unity attests its truth. We feel that we see him as he was. No human being that ever trod the earth has left behind a representation of himself more clear and living, and more certain in its truthfulness, than is that which we possess of the Prophet of Nazareth in Galilee.

From time to time some fresh portrait may appear. Some adventurous imagination, charmed and yet perplexed by the Gospel story, may attempt to reconstruct it in accordance with the spirit of the world. Unable to receive as real the sole example of sinless humanity, it may introduce into the picture touches of the error and infirmity which are not there; and may mistake the awful gleams of the indwelling Godhead for the glimmer of an enthusiasm which deludes and is deluded. The world may read the bold romance, and half commend the creation of fancy. But the creations of fancy perish as they rise, and the Jesus of the Gospels remains; not only as a perfect ideal, but as a *vivid reality*, a representation which appears, after every fresh attempt to change it, more glorious in majesty and beauty, and more conspicuous also for truthfulness and life.

In placing *the statement of the person of Christ* as the first work of the Gospel histories, and as the beginning of the Gospel itself, I speak in accordance with the spirit of those books and of the whole ensuing system of doctrine. Jesus Christ created the Gospel by his work; he preaches the Gospel by his words; but he *is* the Gospel in himself. The expression is but the condensation of a hundred passages of Scripture which declare him to *be* that, which, in more timid but less adequate language, we might say that he *wrought*, or that he *taught*, or that he *gave*. "I am the resurrection and the life."[1] He "is our peace,"[2] he "is our life,"[3] he is "the hope of glory."[4] "He of God is made unto us wisdom, and righteousness, and sanctification, and redemption."[5] and they who are saved "are made partakers of Christ,"[6] not merely of his gifts, whether they be gifts of grace or glory. Is it not indeed

[1] John xi. 25. [2] Eph. ii. 4. [3] Col. iii. 4.
[4] Col. i. 27. [5] 1 Cor. i. 30. [6] Heb. iii. 14.

the distinguishing feature of the Christian system, that it places the foundation of salvation in living relations with a living person, rather than in the adoption of opinions or of habits? that under it the believer is, not the man who maintains the doctrine of the Trinity, or holds "justification by faith," but the man who has "come to" Christ and "abides in" him?

These are the Lord's own words: they are fundamental words in relation to all that is added afterwards: they are, in matter of doctrine, the *beginning* of the Gospel. The writings of the Evangelists do not present to us a scheme of doctrine as to the nature of Christ or as to the work which he does. They present to us the Lord Jesus himself, as he showed himself to men in order to win their confidence and fix their trust. Men learned to know him and to trust him before they fully understood who he was and what he did.

The faith which, in the Gospel stories, we see asked for and given, secured and educated, is a faith that fastens itself on a living Saviour, though it can yet but little comprehend the method or even the nature of the salvation. Thus the New Testament, in giving us these narratives for our first lessons in Christian faith, teaches us that the essential and original nature of that faith lies, not in acceptance of truths which are revealed, but in confidence in a person who is manifested. "He that cometh to me," "He that believeth on me," is the Lord's own account of the child of the new covenant who is the fit recipient of advancing doctrine. Faith, as seen in the Gospels, results not in the first place from the miracles which justify and sustain it, but from the personal impression which appeals to the conscience and the spirit in man. The first disciples believed before a miracle had been shown. It was imputed as a fault, "Except ye see signs and wonders ye will not believe:"[1] and it was a condescension to inferior spiritual sensibilities when the simple words "Believe me"[2] were changed to "Or else believe me for the very works' sake." As it was with those disciples, so also is it with ourselves. The evidential works have their own most important, most necessary office: but the Lord himself is his own evidence, and secures our confidence, love, and adoration, by what he *is* more than what he *does*.

We pass on from the Gospel histories into a dispensation of invisible offices and spiritual relations, and we carry with us the personal knowledge of him by whom these offices and relations are sustained. It is this which secures that they should not be to us a system of ideas and abstractions, of words and names. The Mediator between God and man, the High Priest in the spiritual temple, the King on the unseen throne, is this same Jesus who went in and out among us, whom we have seen sitting in the house at Bethany, or by the well at Sychem, receiving sinners, preaching to the poor, comforting his friends, and suffering little children to come to him. With an acqaintance already formed, a confidence already secured, and a love already awakened, we can pass with a prepared heart to more abstruse revelations of the same Lord, when he is presented as the righteousness of the sinful in the Epistle to the Romans, as the predestined source of life in the Epistle to the Ephesians, as the sacrifice and priest of the new covenant in the Epistle to the Hebrews. Having first

[1] John iv. 48. [2] Ibid. xiv. 11.

known *himself*, we are ready for the Spirit to take of *the things which are his* and show them to us.

II. Our reflections hitherto have turned upon the relation which the Gospel collection bears to the whole New Testament, and we have looked at it as the beginning of a course of doctrine extending through the books which follow. It is now further to be noted, that *its own separate work is itself fulfilled on an apparent plan of progressive development*, which is constituted by the relative characters of the Gospels viewed in the order which they have habitually assumed.

(1.) The collection is divided into two parts by a line of demarcation perceptible to every eye and recognized in every age; the first three Gospels forming the one part and the fourth Gospel the other. The former naturally precedes, and in its effect prepares us for the latter. We are to learn the great lesson of the manifestation of Christ: and here, as in most other subjects, the order of fact is not the order of knowledge. In the order of fact the glory of the divine nature precedes the phenomena of the earthly manifestation; but in the order of knowledge the reverse is true. Events occurring in time, a place in human history, and the external aspect of a life, must supply the antecedent conditions for the higher disclosures. Thus the triple Gospel, which educates us among scenes of earth, prepares us for that which follows. Our minds are led along that very course of thought over which they would have moved if we had been eye-witnesses of the manifestation of Christ, in that we are familiarized with its ordinary aspect and most frequent characteristics, before our thoughts are riveted on those peculiar passages in which the revelation of glory is most concentrated, and which serve to interpret all that we had before felt to be implied.

(2.) Again, if the synoptic Gospels are taken by themselves, we observe, even within the limits of this division, certain orderly steps of advance. Each of these narratives has its own *prevailing character*, whereby it makes its proper contribution to the complete portrait of the Lord: each also has its own *historical associations*, whereby it represents a separate stage in the presentation of Christ to the world. Both the internal characters and the historical associations of the several Gospels have been fully wrought out by recent writers, and are now generally understood. Yet they must be shortly noticed here, for the due elucidation of the statement that the books in combination constitute a progressive course.

The record of St. Matthew, ever recognized as the Hebrew Gospel, is the true *commencement* of the New Testament, showing how it grows out of the Old, and presenting the manifestation of the Son of God not as a detached phenomenon, but as the predestined completion of the long course of historic dispensations. It is the Book of the Generation of Jesus Christ, the Son of *David*, the son of *Abraham*. It founds itself on the ideas of the old covenant. It refers at every step, especially in its earlier chapters, to the former Scriptures, noting how that was fulfilled which was spoken by the prophets. It is a history of *fulfilment*, presenting the Lord as the fulfiller of all righteousness, the fulfiller of the Law and the Prophets, not come to destroy, but to fulfil. It sets him forth as a King and Lawgiver in that kingdom of heaven for which a birthplace and a home had been prepared in Israel: and thus corresponds to that period in the historical course of events when the word was preached to none but to the Jews only.(4)

The Gospel of St. Mark is traditionally connected with St. Peter, who first opened the door of Faith to Gentiles, and has the appearance of being addressed to such a class of converts as it was given to that Apostle to gather, men like the devout soldiers of Cæsarea, in whom the Roman habit of mind was colored by contact with Judaism. It is the Gospel of *action*, rapid, vigorous, vivid. Entering at once on the Lord's official and public career, it bears us on from one mighty deed to another with a peculiar swiftness of movement, and yet with the life of picturesque detail. Power over the visible and invisible worlds, especially as shown in the casting out of devils, is the prominent characteristic of the picture. St. Peter's saying to Cornelius has been well noticed as a fit motto for this Gospel, "God anointed Jesus of Nazareth with the Holy Ghost and with power, who went about doing good and healing all those who were oppressed of the devil." In relation to the expansion of the word from its first home in Jewry to its ultimate prevalence in the whole earth, this Gospel occupies an intermediate position between those of St. Matthew and St. Luke. Its representation of the Lord is disengaged from those close connections with Jewish life and thought which the first Gospel is studious to exhibit, while it is wanting in that breadth of human sympathy and special fitness for the Gentile mind at large which we recognize in the treatise of St. Luke.

This latter Gospel intimates its character in this respect by a genealogy which presents to us not the son of Abraham, but the son of *Adam;* and it carries out the intimation by special notice of our Lord's familiar intercourse with human life, his tender sympathies with human feelings, his large compassion for human woes. The preface, addressed to a Gentile convert, indicating the position of the writer in regard to the facts which he will relate, and speaking in the language of classical composition, shows us at the outset that we have passed from Jewish associations to a stage in the history of the world when its purpose of expansion has been proved, and its character of universality established. The whole tone of this Gospel constitutes it pre-eminently a Gospel for the Gentiles, specially adapted to a Greek mind, then, in some sense, the mind of the world. Its internal character thus accords with its historical position, as the Gospel of St. Paul, written by his close companion, and circulated, we cannot doubt, in the Churches which he founded.

As the book of Acts shows us three stages in the outward progress of the Gospel, first within the bounds of Judaism, then in the work of St. Peter, spreading beyond those limits in the Roman direction, and finally in the ministry of St. Paul, delivered freely and fully to the world; so do the synoptic Gospels, as they stand in the canon, correspond with a singular fitness to those three periods. We are going forward as we pass through them, and are completing the representation of Christ, not by mere repetition or fortuitous variation in our point of view, but in a certain orderly sequence, corresponding to that in which the knowledge of him was historically opened to the world. The evangelical narratives are the proper monuments of a Gospel, which first asserted itself as the true form of Judaism and the legitimate consummation of the old covenant, and then unfolded its relations with the whole race of mankind, and passed into the keeping of a Catholic Church.

(3.) If in traversing the synoptic Gospels we march in the line of a historical advance, it is still more plain that we do so when we pass to the teaching of St. John.

The Gospel of Christ had no sooner completed the conflicts through which it established its relations to Judaism and to the world, than it entered on those profound and subtile, those various and protracted controversies, which turned on the person of Christ. This was the natural course of events, whether we regard the tendencies of human thought, the wiles of the devil, or the government of God. If the revelation of Christ himself (as distinguished from what he taught and what he wrought) is the foundation of the whole Gospel, it would be first to explore this mystery that the activities and subtleties of thought would address themselves; it would be first to destroy this mystery that the assaults of the enemy would be directed; it would be first in securing this mystery that the divine guidance of the Church would be made manifest. One Apostle, the first and the last of the "glorious company," was chosen as the chief instrument for settling human thought, defeating the wiles of the devil, and certifying the witness of God. There was but one moment in which the conditions for such a production could co-exist. It must be after a speculative theosophy had begun to form its language and manifest its aberrations. Yet it must be while the voice of an eye-witness could still be lifted up, to tell what eyes had seen, and ears had heard, and hands had handled of the Word of Life; so that the clearest intuitions of the divinity of Jesus might be forever blended with the plainest testimony of the senses concerning him. Such a moment was secured by the providence which ordained that John should live till the first heresies had shaped themselves. The disciple who first came to Jesus, who followed him most closely, who lay in his bosom, who stood by his cross, who believed when others were confounded, who saw with more penetrating eye the glory which they all beheld, was reserved to complete the written statement of the person of Christ, in a record which has been designated from ancient days as "the Gospel according to the Spirit."

As the other Gospels respectively make prominent the ideas of law, of power, and of grace, so does this present the glory of Christ. "We beheld his glory, the glory as of the Only-begotten of the Father."[1] All the disciples beheld it, but there was one whose pure, lofty, and contemplative spirit fitted him to be the best recipient, and therefore the best exponent, of the sublime disclosure. To him, therefore, the office was assigned, and his Gospel is its fulfilment. He begins, not like his predecessors from an earthly starting-point, from the birth of the son of Adam or the son of Abraham, or the opening of the human ministry, but in the depths of unmeasured eternity and the recesses of the nature of God; and then, bringing the First-begotten into the world, traces with adoring eye the course of word and deed by which he manifested forth his glory, and at last delivers his record to others, "that they may believe that Jesus is the Son of God, and that believing they may have life through his name."[2]

We have now seen that in the three synoptic Gospels the representation of Christ, as he lived and conversed amongst men, is carried on by three successive stages, from its first Jewish aspect and fundamental connection with the old covenant to its most catholic character and adaptation to

[1] John i. 14. [2] Ibid. xx. 31

the Gentile mind; and that these steps correspond to and are connected with the historical stages of advance, by which the Word of God passed from its first home to its destined sphere of influence. We have seen that in the fourth Gospel we rise to a more distinct apprehension of the spiritual mystery involved in the picture which has been presented; and, further, that this advance also is connected with historical conditions, subsequent in time to those under which the preceding books originated. The course of teaching thus produced is according to that principle which places the earthly things as the introduction to the heavenly, and keeps everything in "its own order, first that which is natural, and afterwards that which is spiritual."

And yet these stages of progress are constituted only by differences of degree. There is nothing expanded in one book which has not been asserted in another. Take whatever may seem to you the distinguishing idea of any one of them, and you find a strong expression of it in all the others. The Judaism of St. Matthew reaches out to the calling of the Gentiles; and the catholic spirit of St. Luke falls back upon his Jewish origin. St. John, in exhibiting the divine nature of Christ, exhibits only what the others have everywhere implied and frequently affirmed. "The Johannean conception of Christ," as it has been termed by some who would place it in opposition to preceding representations, is in fact their explication and confirmation. In the former Gospels we behold the Son of God, proclaimed by angels, confessed by devils, acknowledged by the voice of the Father; with authority and power commanding the visible and invisible worlds, and at the central moment of the history transfigured on the holy mount before the eyewitnesses of his majesty. The first word in the Temple declares to his earthly parent his conscious relation to his Father; the last charge to the Apostles founds the Church in the name of the Father, the Son, and the Holy Ghost; while, in the intervening period, some voice of self-revelation more deep than usual is from time to time suffered to fall upon our ears; like that which so many commentators have noticed as a kind of anticipation of the language of St. John, "All things are delivered to me of my Father; and no man knoweth who the Son is but the Father, neither knoweth any man the Father save the Son, and he to whomsoever the Son will reveal him."[1]

On the other hand, it is in the record of St. John that we read words which, if found in another Gospel, would have been eagerly urged as antagonistic to "the Johannean conception." We can imagine what use would then have been made of the argument (John x. 34–36) founded on the text, "I have said ye are gods," or of the assertions, "The words which ye hear are not mine," and "The Father is greater than I." Now, standing in connection with the claim to the incommunicable Name, and with the statements, "All things that the Father hath are mine," and "I and the Father are one," that argument and those assertions cannot be mistaken; but they serve to confirm the unity of that revelation of God manifest in the flesh, of which one aspect is more fully exhibited in one part, and the other aspect in the other part of the Evangelical record.[(5)]

Asserting then the peculiar development which the last Gospel gives to the doctrine of the person of Christ, we also assert that there is no variation from the original conception. The exposition is continuous; the picture is one.

[1] Matt. xi. 27, and Luke x. 22.

From the beginning of St. Matthew to the end of St. John it is one Lord Jesus Christ, as really the Son of Man in the last Gospel as in the first, as really the Son of God in the first Gospel as in the last. Only we find, in passing under the teaching of St. John, that here the great mystery shows more vivid and mature; that the intuitions of it have become more conscious and clear, and the assertions of it more definite and indisputable; that we have advanced from the simple observation of facts to the state of retrospection and reflection, and that we have attained to the formation of a language fitted to the highest conceptions of him who is the Only-begotten of the Father, the Life, and the Light, and the Truth, and the Word Eternal.

Such is the character of the Gospel collection, regarded as an exposition of the doctrine of the person of Christ. As a scheme characterized by unity and progress it has obviously the appearance of design: and the appearance of design is an argument for its reality.

But *whose* design is this, which appears not in the separate books, but in the collection taken as a whole? The agents were severed from each other, and wrote as their respective turns of mind and historical circumstances determined. Where then was the presiding mind which planned the whole, and, in qualifying and employing the chosen agents, divided to every man severally as he would? By the voice of the Church as a body, by the ever-accumulating consent of her several members, an unchanging answer comes down from age to age. The Spirit of the Lord is here.

Yes! the Spirit was to testify of Jesus, and the fourfold Gospel is his permanent testimony. In it he has provided that the foundations of our faith should be laid in the region where the foundations of all human knowledge lie, namely, in the evidence of the senses, in that which "eyes have seen, ears have heard, and hands have handled of the Word of Life." He has provided that the object of our faith should be known to us as he was known to those who saw him, that he should be clearly known by the simplicity, fully known by the variety, and certainly known by the unity, of the narratives which give to the world the perpetual and only representation of its Redeemer. Finally, he has provided that the representation should be completed by a progressive course of teaching, which first familiarizes us with the conversation of our Lord among men in its general and ordinary aspect, and then admits us to the more concentrated study of the glory and the mystery, which had already made themselves felt at every step.

I have only to add, that the divine teaching thus given, even when viewed separately, has the appearance of being not a whole scheme ending in itself, but a part of a larger scheme. I mean that the *general effect* of the manifestation which is made in the Gospels is such as almost necessitates farther disclosures.

One shining with the glory of the Only-begotten of the Father, but clothed in the poverties and infirmities of man, has walked before us in power and weakness, in majesty and woe. He has come close to us, and drawn us close to him; has touched every chord of our hearts: has secured our implicit trust, and become the object of adoration and love: then he has hung upon a cross, has sunk into a grave, has risen, has ascended, and is gone. It was a brief dispensation, and is finished once for all. What did it mean? What has it done? What are our relations with him now? and in what way has this brief appearance affected our position before God and the state and destiny of the soul? What is the nature of the redemption which he has wrought, of the salvation which he has brought, of the kingdom of God which he has opened to all believers?

These were questions left for the Disciples when Jesus was gone; and, when the reader of the Gospel story reaches its close, these questions remain for him. The Disciples would recall what their Master had spoken, in order to gather the whole result of the words of his lips. The reader also will review that personal teaching of Christ which is interwoven with his visible manifestation, and will ask whether it gives an answer to the questions which the manifestation suggests; whether it does so fully or partially, as a final communication, or as the commencement of information to be completed afterwards. This is the subject which will next claim our attention, as the first step in the inquiry, how the Christian doctrine was added to the Christian facts —the divine interpretation to the divine intervention.

The relations between these two parts of the Gospel have now in some measure come into view. We have seen that the evangelical narrative creates the want and gives the pledge of an evangelical doctrine; that it also deposits its material and provides its safeguard.

a. The narrative creates the *want*, in that it leaves the mind of the reader in a state of desire and expectation, since the stupendous facts which it recites cannot but suggest anxious inquiries which wait for clear replies, and vast speculations which demand a firm direction.

b. And this want seems to carry with it the *pledge* that it is raised in order to be satisfied. We feel sure that God has not given us the external manifestation of his Son, and then left the questions which arise out of it unanswered and the hopes which it suggests undefined. In the fulness and vividness of the record of the facts we find an implied assurance, that their purposes and results shall also be made clear, and receive in their proper place their own proper exposition.

c. Again, the history deposits the *material* of the doctrine; for that material is nothing else than Christ manifest in the flesh — his incarnation, his obedience, his holiness, love, grace, and truth, his death and passion, his resurrection and ascension, and then, beyond these, his glorified life, and his coming and his kingdom, in which the past history finds its necessary and predicted issues. These, brethren, are the topics of the evangelical teaching, and the constituent elements of the truth, seeing that in this manifestation of the Son of God all that men had known before has received its full illustration and its final seal, and that which they had not known has been once for all revealed. All that is to be learned is comprised within this circle. The deep mine of truth lies beneath this spot. "In him (as the mystery of God) are hid all the treasures of wisdom and knowledge."[1]

d. Lastly, the narrative provides the *safeguard* of the doctrine. Before we arrive at the latter form of teaching, we have been secured against its possible dangers, having been already taught in the most effective way to feel that our trust is not in a name which we learn, but in a person whom we know; not in a scheme of salvation, but in a living Saviour. I cannot say how strongly I feel the value of the Gospel narrative in this last point of view; and I feel it most when I observe the effect of other methods,

[1] Col. ii. 3.

which have trained the minds of disciples mainly by schemes of doctrine without the admixture in its due proportion of the ever fresh and healthful element of history. Blessed be the wisdom of God, which has ordered the teaching of the New Testament upon its actual plan, laying first the living knowledge of the Lord Jesus as the broadest and safest basis for doctrine and instruction in righteousness. The order thus observed in the written word teaches how the knowledge of Christ will best be opened out to every single soul. He only is duly prepared for more abstract revelations of the nature of the redeeming work and of its present and future issues, in whose heart the past manifestation in the flesh is clearly reflected, and who thus has worthily received into his own soul "the beginning of the Gospel of Jesus Christ the Son of God."

LECTURE III.

THE GOSPELS.

HOW SHALL WE ESCAPE, IF WE NEGLECT SO GREAT SALVATION, WHICH AT THE FIRST BEGAN TO BE SPOKEN BY THE LORD?—*Heb.* *ii.* 3.

From age to age this question has fulfilled its office. Men, trusting in their immunity from criminal acts, have found themselves confronted by an accusation which they could not answer, and convicted of guilt of which they had never thought. Still may this question reach one heart after another amongst ourselves, and flash the sense of sin and ruin on those who even now, and even here, are practically neglecting so great salvation!

Not, however, on this question, but on the following words, have I now to fix your attention; words which are added to aggravate the sin of that neglect, and to illustrate the certainty of a corresponding retribution; but which do so by the mention of a fact which falls into our present line of thought at the point which we have now reached. This "so great salvation began to be spoken by the Lord, and was confirmed unto us by them that heard him; God also bearing them witness by signs and wonders, and gifts of the Holy Ghost, according to his own will."

It began to be spoken *by the Lord*. The word of the old covenant is repeatedly declared to have been "received by the disposition of angels"[1]—"ordained by angels"[2]—"spoken by angels."[3] The ministering spirits, the mes-

[1] Acts vii. 53. [2] Gal. iii. 19. [3] Heb. ii. 2

sengers and servants of the Lord, were employed to introduce the preparatory system. On the other hand, the salvation of the new covenant is introduced, not by the servants, but by the Lord in person. His introduction of it was not confined to providing its conditions and foundations, by the manifestation of himself, and by the redemption which he wrought. He was the messenger and teacher of this salvation, as well as its author and giver. It was fully wrought by the Lord; but, besides that, it began to be "*spoken*" by the Lord, its announcement coming first from his own lips. Yet this personal speaking was only a certain stage in the course of its publication. "It *began* to be spoken by the Lord,"[1] and when he ceased to speak the word was not yet completed. It was to be cleared and assured to the world by those that heard him; who, having been educated and commissioned by him for the purpose, proceeded to preach the Gospel with the Holy Ghost sent down from heaven, and with adequate proofs of the co-attestation of God.

This account of the personal ministry of the Lord Jesus, as an initiatory stage of the word of salvation, gives me the subject of which I have now to treat. Evidently it is one of the very highest importance in its bearings on the subsequent stages of doctrine; on which we shall enter in a very different spirit, if we consider the word spoken by the Lord in person as a *finished word*, or if we regard it as a *word begun*.

As steps which may be of use towards attaining a true view of the case, I would lay down the following propositions.

[1] Ἀρχὴν λαβοῦσα λαλεῖσθαι διὰ τοῦ Κυρίου.

First, The teaching of the Lord in the Gospels *includes the substance of all christian doctrine, but does not bear the character of finality.* Secondly, The teaching of the Lord in the Gospels *is a visibly progressive course, but on reaching its highest point announces its own incompleteness, and opens another stage of instruction.*

I. 1. The teaching of the Lord in the Gospels *includes the substance of all christian doctrine.* Never was teaching more *natural* than his. It was drawn forth by occasions as they arose. It shaped itself to the character, the words, and the acts of those whom he met in the highway of the world. It borrowed its imagery from the circumstances and scenery of the moment. Such teaching as this would *not* seem likely to embrace the whole circle of truth. We should expect to find it partial and fragmentary; full in some points, deficient in others, according as the occasions for evoking it had or had not arisen.

Yet surely the whole course of the manifestation of the Son of God would be governed not by accident, but by a special divine predestination: and there must have been a providential appointment of the fittest occasions and the most perfect conditions, in order that he who came from God to speak the words of God might adequately accomplish his mission. Then the general state of the religious atmosphere at the time of his appearing, the strongly discriminated developments of opinion in Pharisees and Sadducees, the condition of individuals who came across his path, the scenes and circumstances in which he met them, were all prepared by divine governance, to further the effectual fulfilment of his mission as the teacher of men. Thus it came to pass, that not only in set discourses (which seldom occur), but in transient conversations and sudden replies, in words drawn forth by the appeals of the wretched, by the temptations of enemies or by the errors of disciples, in strong denunciations of the wicked or in tender consolations of the weak, the mind of Christ has been expressed on all points, and the store of divine sentences is full.

Shall I enter into detail, and begin to show how the whole argument on justification in the Epistle to the Romans is involved in the assertion, that "the Son of Man was lifted up, that he that believeth on him should not perish but have everlasting life"?[1] — how the exposition of the Christian standing in the Epistle to the Galatians is comprehended in the words, "The servant abideth not in the house forever, but the son abideth ever. If the son make you free ye shall be free indeed"?[2] — how the sacrificial doctrine of the Epistle to the Hebrews is implied in all its parts by the words, "This is my blood of the new covenant, which is shed for you and for many for the remission of sins"?[3] Though such proof in detail is here impossible, it would yet be easy to show that every doctrine expanded in the Epistles roots itself in some pregnant saying in the Gospels; and that the first intimation of every truth, revealed to the holy Apostles by the Spirit, came first from the lips of the Son of Man. In each case the later revelation may enlarge the earlier, may show its meaning and define its application, but the earlier revelation stands behind it still, and we owe our first knowledge of every part of the new covenant to those personal communications in which the salvation began to be spoken by the Lord.

[1] John iii. 14, 15. [2] John viii. 35, 36. [3] Matt. xxvi. 28.

"In all things he was to have the pre-eminence,"[1] in speaking as well as in acting, not only as the Life, but also as the Light of men. The more we study the records of that short ministry in the flesh, the more we are impressed with the fact that all the past and all the future are gathered up in it. Past inspired teaching here finds its meaning interpreted and its authority sealed, whilst (so to speak) the several chapters of future inspired teaching are opened by pregnant summaries and certified by anticipatory sanctions. That is indeed a time "of large discourse, looking before and after," and the words of Prophets on the one side, and of Apostles on the other, are forever justified and maintained by the words of him who came between them.

There was nothing then on the lips of the preachers of the Gospel, but what had been "begun to be spoken" by its first preacher; and in following to their utmost the words of the Apostles we are still within the compass of the words of the Lord Jesus.

2. Yet those words *do not bear the character of finality.* The doctrine delivered in the Gospels appears to need, and to promise, further explanations, combinations, and developments. The character of that ministry on the whole is introductory. It is so in its *form*, in its *method*, and in its *substance.*

a. Our Lord's general teaching, in regard to its *form*, is cast in the mould of parable or proverb. So it appears more especially in the first three Gospels as compared with the fourth: and it is agreed on all hands that the former represent the ordinary course of the teaching of Jesus; and

1 ἐν πᾶσιν αὐτὸς πρωτεύων.

that the latter purposely collects into one view those stronger assertions of divine mysteries, which were made on particular occasions, and which, when thus combined, form for us a more advanced stage of revelation. Yet in St. John also the characteristic form of parable continues, though its visible diminution corresponds with the increased intensity of revealing light.

There can be no need to exhibit the fact of this prevailing character of our Lord's discourse. It is to be noticed, not only in the large amount of professed parables, but in the general habit of proverbial sayings, that is, sayings which glance by us, as condensed and momentary parables, suggesting much that it would take long to tell, or, at least, sayings which have more or less the shape and air of proverbs, complete in themselves, terse and pointed, fashioned for common memory and common use, meaning more than they say, and, by strong antithesis or seeming paradox, fitted to arouse reflection, and to fix on the mind some principle of thought or conduct. This characteristic of our Lord's teaching does not exist in that of his servants. It is peculiar and distinctive; and not without reason, for it falls in with that character of germinating *fulness* which has been already ascribed to the personal ministry of Christ; and not less plainly with that character of *initiation* which is now to be asserted.

It is of the essence of proverbial speech that it detaches itself from particular occasions, that it has a capacity for various applications, and a fitness for permanent use, and embraces large meaning within narrow limits. It therefore fitted well the lips which were to utter the great principles of Christian thought, and to leave them amongst men for all times and occasions. Yet this form of teaching belongs to the *introduction* of knowledge. It seems intended to set the mind working, and to rouse the spirit of inquiry by partial or disguised discoveries of truth. "To them that are without," said our Lord, "all these things are done in parables;"[1] intimating that the use of that form of instruction is appropriate to the preliminary and probationary stage. In its fullest degree it belongs originally to those that are without, though, by means of light afterwards afforded, it continues to minister large instruction to those that are within. To the multitude our Lord's teaching was mainly of this character: to his disciples it was obviously less so. To them "it was given to know the mysteries of the kingdom of God, but to others in parables."[2] Yet to them also, through all their time of training, we see that this mode of speech is largely used, and when the personal intercourse is about to close they receive the assurance that the teaching of the future will herein differ from that of the past: "These things have I spoken unto you in proverbs, but the time cometh when I shall no more speak unto you in proverbs, but I shall show you plainly of the Father."[3] The words remain as a sufficient testimony that the peculiar character of language, in which the salvation began to be spoken by the Lord, is a mark of an introductory stage, and, so far as it prevails, is both a sign that the time for showing plainly is not yet come, and a pledge that it is to follow.

b. As the form of the teaching leads to this conclusion, so also does its *method*. It is seemingly to a great degree

[1] Mark iv. 11. ἐκείνοις τοῖς ἔξω—yet certainly not to *keep* them without, but as the appropriate means to draw them within.

[2] Luke viii. 10.

[3] John xvi. 25.

a method of chances and occasions; carried on by words suited to the moment, by separate addresses, or replies to particular persons, and by explanations added to particular acts. It is moreover in these communications, rather than in the deliberate discourses, that the higher revelations of his Gospel are for the most part contained. When "he opened his mouth and taught" in the Sermon on the Mount, he delivered to those who were entering his kingdom the great *principles of moral righteousness*. But it is from words dropped as it were in a private conversation by night, or in collision with the provocations of unbelievers, or amid sighs and sorrows by the grave of a friend, that we derive our plainest assurances of the *mysteries of his salvation*. While we gather up the precious things of his ordinary discourses, we are made sensible that other truths are implied, deeper than those which are announced, and from time to time the words which assert those deeper truths break with a kind of suddenness on our ears. It would hardly appear likely that such a mode of teaching was intended to be final; rather we should expect it to prove (as in fact it did) the prefatory announcement of a coming system of truth, in which the several sayings would discover their cohesion and the condensed assertions would expand into their fulness.

c. If the form and method of the personal teaching of Jesus suggest the conclusion, that it was meant to be, not the whole of his teaching to men, but only the initiatory stage of it, that conclusion becomes more sure when we come to consider the *substance* of the doctrine itself.

The doctrine bears a double character. It is, first, the clearing, restoring, and perfecting of truth already known; and it is, secondly, the revealing of a mysterious economy which had not yet been divulged. It is, I suppose, obvious to every reader of the Gospels, that the doctrine contained in them is much more full and explicit in the first of these characters than it is in the second; that all which belongs to human duty and character comes out habitually to view in the clearest light, while the discoveries of that secret scheme of things, by which the divine purposes are worked out, are either made by implication, or are marked by a certain brevity and reserve. This fact is generally recognized, and especially by those minds which shrink from the more mysterious parts of revelation. These fall back upon the Lord's own teaching in the Gospels, as containing more to which they can cordially assent, or at least less which troubles and perplexes them, than they find in the writings of his followers. All that troubles and perplexes them is indeed there; but the restricted measure of its exposition allows them more easily to ignore its presence. Such men fly to the Sermon on the Mount, and linger over parables and discourses, which instruct us in the great original truths of the fatherhood of God, of heartfelt prayer, of love and forgiveness, of lowliness and truth, of obedience and self-sacrifice, of confidence in pardoning mercy, and of faith (yet only general and preliminary) in him whom God hath sent.

It is indeed true that in passing through the synoptic Gospels we meet with few express and definite assertions of the real nature and effects of the mediatorial work of Christ; and if we drop out of notice those few strong sayings, andare content to take the lowest meaning of every expression that sounds ambiguous, and are resolutely insensible to the suggestion of typical miracles and to the implications contained in the whole history, we may perhaps arrive at the Gospel of St. John with no higher convictions than were expressed by the inquirer, whom we there find uttering the dubious acknowledgment, "Master, we know that thou art a *teacher* come from God."[1]

But having acknowledged this much, we must from this point acknowledge much more. We find that the Gospel on which we have entered has collected for us the scattered sayings, in which, from time to time, our Lord asserted his highest offices, and opened the mystery of his work. One after another the great testimonies concerning himself fall on our ears: yet, in regard to every one of them, we are made to feel that the intimations given are at the time beyond the apprehensions of the hearers, and this not only on account of the dulness of the particular persons, but because the testimonies imply events which have not yet happened, and are fragments of a revelation for which the hour is not yet come. Glance through a few of these sayings: The heavens open, and the angels ascending and descending on the Son of Man;[2] the Temple destroyed and raised up again in three days;[3] the birth of water and the Spirit;[4] the Son of Man who came from heaven, who goes to heaven, and who is in heaven;[5] the lifting up like the serpent in the wilderness, that men may not perish;[6] the water which he will give, springing up into everlasting life;[7] the eating the flesh and drinking the blood as the means of everlasting life and of being raised up at the last day.[8] These sayings, and many others like them, are uttered to hearers whose perplexity is made apparent, and are

[1] ἔτι ἀπὸ Θεοῦ ἐλήλυθας διδάσκαλος.

[2] John i. 51. [3] Ibid. ii. 19. [4] Ibid. iii. 5.
[5] Ibid. iii. 13. [6] Ibid. iii. 14. [7] Ibid. iv. 14.
[8] Ibid. vi. 54.

at the time left unexplained, to await the light which they are to receive from future events and later discoveries. This (if I may so call it) anticipatory character of our Lord's teaching, with regard to the work which he came to fulfil, strikes us most forcibly, when we compare his mode of speaking on the subject with the full and explicit language which becomes familiar to us in the writings of his Apostles.

And if this account of one part of his teaching be true, an evident consequence follows in regard to the other part. Grant that the discoveries of the redeeming work of Christ are in any measure restricted and deferred, and it follows that a large part of the teaching on human duty must be restricted and deferred in proportion. Instructions in faith in himself must wait for their perfecting, until the things to be believed concerning him have grown clear. Instructions in our relations to God (whether bearing on the hope of a penitent or on the confidence of a child) have not obtained their completion while the grounds of forgiveness and acceptance are in any manner obscure. Finally, instructions on duty and character must be deficient in some of their most important elements, while the motives which flow from redemption cannot be assumed as recognized, because Jesus has not yet died; while the life in the Spirit, and the power of the resurrection, and the citizenship in heaven, cannot be realized, because Jesus has not yet revived, risen, and ascended.

In illustration of these assertions I will instance the treatment of the two doctrines of *the forgiveness of sins* and *the success of prayer*. We know how intimately in the evangelical system these two doctrines are associated with the personal agency of our Redeemer, the one with his atoning sacrifice, the other with his priestly mediation. But it is certain that in his own teaching on earth they are *not* so treated. Other truths concerning them are brought forward when these are absent.

Take the first example. "*Forgive*, and ye shall be forgiven;"[1] "Her sins, which are many, are forgiven, *for she loved much;*"[2] "I forgave thee all that debt *because thou desiredst me;*"[3] "He smote upon his breast, saying, God be merciful to me *a sinner*,"[4] and then "went down to his house justified rather than the other." Lastly, in the great parable of forgiveness the erring son simply *returns*, and the father falls on his neck and kisses him. "Father," says he, "I have sinned against heaven and before thee," and straightway he is clothed with the best robe, and has the ring on his hand, and the shoes on his feet. "He was dead and is alive again: he was lost, and is found." There is no mention of any intercessor, no typical hint of sacrifice or other atonement, no condition anywhere supposed, but what is included in "because thou desiredst me," or in the presence of penitence and tenderness of heart, and the absence of an unforgiving spirit towards others. Yet at other times there fall from the Lord's own lips some few words at least which reveal *himself* as the channel, and *his blood* as the purchase, of the forgiveness which he preaches so freely. "The Son of Man has power on earth to forgive sins;"[5] "My blood shed for many for the remission of sins."[6] These sayings give a momentary insight into the depths of the subject, and disclose something of the mysterions *means* by which forgiveness has been procured, and through which, when once revealed, it must be sought. It is evident that

[1] Luke vi. 37. [2] Ibid. vii. 47. [3] Matt. xviii. 32.
[4] Luke xviii. 13. [5] Matt. ix. 6. [6] Ibid. xxvi. 28.

such a revelation cannot remain as a mere associated idea, that it must become *fundamental*, and give a peculiar and distinctive character to the Christian doctrine of the forgiveness of sins. But we see that it is not wrought out in the Gospels. Must we not then expect that this will yet be done? and that, in some future stage of divine teaching, we shall find the word "Forgive and ye shall be forgiven" elevated and opened into "Forgiving one another as God *for Christ's sake* hath forgiven you,"[1] and the hope of forgiveness placed forever on its true basis of faith in him, "in whom we have redemption *through his blood*, even the forgiveness of sins."[2]

Again, take the doctrine of *acceptance and success in prayer*. How earnest and how strong are our Lord's declarations on this subject! It is needless to rehearse them, but these precious assurances are here connected only with the earnestness, importunity, and simplicity of the worshippers, and with a general faith in the Father's will to give good things to those that ask him. We might be ready to say, "The whole instruction amounts to this,—Dismiss all heathen and all Pharisaic notions on this subject. Go simply to God as your Father. Ask, and ye shall receive." Yet he who has taught us, before he ceases to speak, adds something more. At the highest point of his teaching we hear him say, "No man cometh unto the Father *but by me;*[3] "If ye shall ask anything *in my name I* will do it."[4] Here is an immense accession of revelation, which, when fully comprehended, must give its character to the whole Christian doctrine and to the whole Christian habit of

[1] Eph. iv. 32.
[2] Ibid. i. 7.
[3] John xiv. 6.
[4] Ibid. xvi. 23.

prayer. But if we are ever to see this consequence wrought out by divine teaching, we must find it in some future stage of instruction, in which the access to the Father by the Son, and the new and living way which he has consecrated for us, and the offices of the High Priest over the house of God, shall be recognized as the true grounds of the full assurance of faith, for him who draws near to God in prayer.

The argument then stands thus. The doctrine of the Gospel includes special revelations which *must from their nature become the foundations of moral and spiritual life.* But in the doctrine of the Gospels they are not *so* treated, nor indeed could they be, since the revelations themselves are chiefly anticipatory allusions to facts which have not yet taken place. In these revelations the teaching culminates rather than commences. They are the point at which it arrives, not that from which it starts. The doctrine does not therefore bear the character of finality. We expect another stage, in which these special revelations shall be not only cleared and combined, but shall hold that *fundamental place* in the whole system of instruction which they tend inevitably to assume. And thus, from the consideration of the substance and proportions of the doctrine in the Gospels, as well as from the observation of its form and method, I conclude that I am here only in an initiatory stage of divine teaching, and that another part of the course must lie before me.

II. But I am not left to draw this conclusion. The doctrine of the Gospels not only looks as if it were to be followed by another stage of teaching, but declares that such is the fact. I come to my second proposition, that the personal teaching of the Lord is *a visibly progressive system, which, on reaching its highest point, declares its own incompleteness, and refers us to another stage of instruction.*

1. Place side by side the first discourse in St. Matthew and the last in St. John, and the truth of the first part of this proposition is at once apparent, namely, that the personal teaching of the Lord is *a visibly progressive system.* The Sermon on the Mount at the opening of the ministry, and the address in the upper room delivered at its close, are separated from each other, not only by difference of circumstance and feeling, but as implying on the part of the hearers wholly different stages in the knowledge of truth. There is a greater interval between these two discourses than there is between the teaching of the Gospels as a whole and that of the Epistles.

The first discourse is the voice of a minister of the circumcision, clearing and confirming the divine teaching given to the fathers. Blessings, laws, and promises are alike founded on the Old Testament language, which the speaker at the same time adopts and interprets. He keeps in a line with the past, while he makes a clear step in advance. He gives, not so much a new code, as a new edition of the old one. The word of authority, "*I* say unto you," is directed not to destroy but to fulfil. It is the authority of the original lawgiver, clearing up his own intentions, and disallowing the perversions of men. As plainly as the first discourse links itself to the past, so plainly does the last discourse reach on to the future. If the one reverts to what was said in old time, the other casts the mind forward on a day of knowledge which is dawning and a new teacher who is coming. In passing from the one point to the other, we have left behind us the language and associations of the Old Testament: we have entered a new world of thought, and hear a new language which is being created for its exigencies. What makes the thought and the language new? One single fact; namely, that the true relation of the Lord Jesus to the spiritual life of his people is now in a measure revealed. "Ye believe in God, *believe also in me:*" — this is the keynote of the whole address. And in the same strain it continues, "No man cometh unto the Father but by me;" "Abide in me and I in you;" "Without me ye can do nothing." How foreign would such words have been in the Sermon on the Mount! We are not unprepared for them here, though even here they mean more than can be yet understood. I do not speak of single expressions, but of the whole doctrine on faith and prayer, and love, and service, and hope, and life. All subjects have here assumed their distinctively Christian character: they are "*in Christ Jesus.*" The faith fixes itself on *him*, and on the Father *through him.* The prayer is "*in his name.*" The love is a response to *his* love. The service is the fruit of union with *him.* The hope is that of being with *him* where he is; to *abide in him* is the secret of life, safety, fruitfulness, and joy; and the guiding power of this new state is not the explanation of a law, but the gift of the Holy Ghost the Comforter. Compare these ideas with those which characterize the first Gospel teaching, and you see how far you have been carried from the point at which you started. You see how much must have intervened in the gradual revelation of Christ, and in the gradual advance of his teaching, before such a stage of doctrine could be reached.

And much *had* intervened. To show *how* much, it would be necessary to trace through all the Gospel record the unfolding of the salvation, as it began to be spoken by the Lord, and the steps by which it was brought about, that the

Master and the disciples should become the Saviour and the believers, and that the external hearing and following should pass into the mysterious relations of an inward and spiritual union. It is enough to recall the fact that, through all the works of mercy, the corrections of error, and the instructions in righteousness, a deeper lesson yet is sinking into the minds of his hearers, in the growing sense of a profound and ineffable relation borne by him to the human race and to every human soul. He makes it felt, that he stands before men as the one object on which faith must fasten, as the one who has power on earth to forgive sins, who is come to seek and to save that which is lost, who gives rest to the heavy laden, as the giver of eternal life, as the quickener of whom he will, as the bread which came down from heaven that a man may eat thereof and not die, as giving his flesh for the life of the world, his life a ransom for many, his blood as the blood of the new covenant shed for many for the remission of sins. Testimonies like these gather as we advance; and while the Lord in his ordinary teaching fulfils his mission as the expounder of the laws, and the example of the character, and the prophet of the destinies of the kingdom of God, he discloses at the same time by these scattered sayings a far deeper and more fundamental relation to that kingdom and to all its several members.

But while these disclosures are yet in progress they are suddenly cut off. The ministry must end: the hour is come. We enter the upper room, and attend the last discourse, which is the close and the consummation of the teaching of the Lord on earth.

2. We turn, then, to that portion of the word of God which extends from the beginning of the 14th to the end of the 17th chapter of St. John. There, in words most simple

but unfathomably deep, addressed first to men and then to God, there flow forth the thoughts which belong to that hour. Oh tender, solemn words! Oh words of majesty and love, of divine sorrow and joy! words for the saddest moments, the loftiest moments, the last moments of life! Not in the cold spirit of one who would prove a point do I turn to them now, though it be indeed to decide a question. But what a question! Not one affecting some single doctrine which some text in the discourse may touch, but one affecting all the doctrine before and after, all that began to be spoken by the Lord and was confirmed to us by them that heard him. It is the question whether the point which we have reached is *final* or *central:* whether the true teaching of God here reaches a close or effects a transition. There is no uncertainty in the answer, for to give that answer is one main purpose of the discourse. The Lord speaks to the occasion. He would have it understood to what point in the progress of his teaching we are come, and what is the relation between that which is now ending and that which is about to begin.

At the first glance it is plain that the character of the discourse is distinctly *transitional;* that it announces not an *end*, but a *change;* and that, in closing one course of teaching, it at the same time opens another. As the first discourse linked the personal teaching of Christ to the Law and the Prophets which went before it, so the last discourse links that teaching to the dispensation of the Spirit, which is to come after it. The fact on which the first is founded is that the *Law* of God has been given to men as the guide to *righteousness;* the fact on which the last is founded is that *Jesus* himself has now been presented to men as the object of *faith.* And as it was intimated in the one case that the lesson of righteousness was yet incomplete, and was to be perfected by Jesus himself, so it is intimated in the other that the lesson of faith is yet incomplete, and is to be perfected by the Holy Ghost whom he will send.

First, the narrative is careful to show us that this lesson of faith had been imperfectly *learned.* The auditors are the men whom the Lord had chosen and trained, and who had watched most closely the whole course of his manifestation. Yet, as he proceeds, what do we hear? "Lord, we know not whither thou goest, and how can we know the way?" "Show us the Father and it sufficeth us." "How is it that thou wilt manifest thyself unto us and not unto the world?" "What is this that he saith? we cannot tell what he saith." By such voices of faint and partial apprehension or of sore perplexity, we learn how far the teaching of the past had gone with them, in regard to those truths which were being then set forth.

But it might be, notwithstanding, that the course of divine instruction *was* complete, and that events yet to come and reflection on the past would be sufficient to open to them its meaning. Not thus does the Lord reply. Mingled with sad reflections, that he has been so long time with them and that yet they have not known him, he gives the consoling assurance that their instruction in the truth is not yet ended. A part of it is over, but only a part; and a part which had its hindrances as well as its helps. The presence of Christ in the flesh had been a help to what they had already learned; it was a hindrance to what they had now to learn.[6] While he sat there before them in the body, it was hard to understand the mystery of a spiritual union. That hindrance is to be removed; "It is expedient for you that I go away"

Then the teaching which he had given them must close. Yes, but another teaching shall be substituted; which shall be also *his*, though suited to the new relations which he shall bear to them in his glorified state. "It is expedient for you that I go away, for if I go not away the Comforter will not come unto you, but if I depart I will send him unto you." Then follow those precious promises of the coming and office and work of the Holy Ghost, which expand their fulfilment over the whole Church and throughout all ages. But while it is clear that, in the way of extension and of inference, many of the words allow and invite this wider application, it is far more evident that in their first intention they are directly addressed to those who heard them, and meant to meet the question of the particular crisis which had then arrived.[1]

[1] "I will pray the Father, and he shall give you another Comforter, that he may abide with you forever; even the Spirit of truth; whom the world cannot receive, because it seeth him not, neither knoweth him: but ye know him, for he dwelleth with you, and shall be in you. I will not leave you comfortless, I will come unto you." John xiv. 16–18. "At that day ye shall know that I am in the Father, and ye in me, and I in you." Ver. 20. "These things have I spoken to you, while abiding with you; but the Comforter, which is the Holy Ghost, whom the Father will send in my name, he shall teach you all things, and bring all things to your remembrance, whatsoever I have said unto you." Ver. 25, 26. "When the Comforter is come, he shall testify of me." xv. 26. "He shall reprove the world of sin, and of righteousness, and of judgment: of sin, because they believe not on me; of righteousness, because I go to my Father, and ye see me no more; of judgment, because the prince of this world is judged. I have yet many things to say unto you, but ye cannot bear them now. Howbeit, when he, the Spirit of truth, is come, he shall guide you

No more distinct assurance could have been given that those future teachers of the world were not then at the end, but only at a certain point in the progress of their education, and that a teaching remained for them, which should both continue and surpass that which they had already received.

But had they not heard the truth from their Lord! Yes; and it was to be the office of the Spirit to recall to their minds the truth which they had heard, as the text and substance of their future knowledge. "He shall bring all things to your remembrance, whatsoever I have said unto you." But though in the teaching of Jesus all the truth might be *implied*, it was not all *opened;* therefore the Holy Ghost was to add that which had not been delivered, as well as to recall that which had been already spoken. There is an evident contrast intended, with regard to extent of knowledge, between "*these things* which I have spoken while yet present with you," and "*all* things which he shall teach you." Nay, there is the plainest assertion which could be made, that things were to be said afterwards which had not been said then; and those not few but *many*—("I have yet many things to say unto you") —not of secondary importance but of the *highest moment* ("Ye cannot bear them now."[1]) They are things of such a kind as would now weigh down and oppress your minds, seeing that they surpass your present powers of spiritual apprehension. But these many and weighty things shall

into all truth; for he shall not speak of himself, but whatsoever he shall hear that shall he speak; and he shall show you things to come. He shall glorify me, for he shall receive of mine, and shall show it unto you" xvi. 8–14.

[1] οὐ δύνασθε βαστάζειν.

not be left untold: "When he, the Spirit of truth, is come, he shall guide you into all the truth." He shall guide you,[1] as by successive steps and continuous direction, into the whole of that truth[2] of which the commencements have now been given; and especially into the highest and central part of it. For it is also made plain on what *subject* this light shall be poured, and into what mysteries this guidance shall lead. "He shall testify of *me;*" "he shall glorify *me;*" "he shall take of *mine* and show it unto you;" "at that day ye shall know that *I am in the Father, and ye in me, and I in you.*" Not then for some secondary matters (details of Church order or relations of Jews and Gentiles) was this light and witness of the Holy Ghost reserved (though to these questions also the divine guidance extended), but rather for the great and central mystery of godliness, embracing the nature, work, and offices of Jesus Christ, his mediatorial relations to the Father and to the Church, the redemption of men by his blood, and the salvation of men by his life. But instead of attempting to enumerate these great ideas, it were better to comprehend them all in his own vast and unexplained expression, "He shall take of mine,[3] and shall show it unto you."

We have now reviewed the teaching of our Lord in the flesh, in order to draw from it an answer to this question, "Is the revelation of the great salvation given to us in that teaching to be considered as final and complete?" The answer has been, "No! *It has not the appearance* of being final, and it *explicitly declares* that it is not complete. When it was ended, it was to be followed by a new

[1] ὁδηγήσει. [2] εἰς πᾶσαν τὴν ἀλήθειαν [3] ἐκ τοῦ ἐμοῦ λήψεται

testimony from God, in order that many things might be spoken which had not been spoken then."

The testimony came; the things were spoken; and in the apostolic writings we have their enduring record. In those writings we find the fulfilment of an expectation which the Gospels raised, and recognize the performance of a promise which the Gospels gave. If we do *not*, the word of salvation, which began to be spoken by the Lord, has never been finished for us. Then, not only would the end be wanting, but the beginning would become obscure. The lessons of holiness would still shine in their own pure light, and the rebukes of human error would show in their severe outlines; but the words which open by anticipation the mystery of the great salvation, flashing sometimes on its deep foundations, sometimes on its lofty summits, would but dazzle and confuse our sight; and we should be tempted to turn from their discoveries, as from visions which had no substance, or from enigmas which we could not interpret.

And so in fact *they* treat the personal teaching of Christ who give not its due honor to the subsequent witness of his Spirit, regarding the apostolic writings as only Petrine, Pauline, or Alexandrian versions of the Christian doctrine, interesting records of the views of individuals or schools of opinion concerning the salvation which Jesus began to speak. No! the words of our Lord are not honored (as these men seem to think) by being thus isolated; for it is an isolation which separates them from other words which also are his own, words given by him in that day when he no longer spake in proverbs, but showed his servants plainly of the Father. The brief communications in which the salvation began to be spoken by the Lord must lose half their glory, if a mist and darkness be cast over that later teaching which was ordained to throw its reflex light upon them.

Our thoughts have now arrived at the point where the day of "speaking in proverbs" changes into the day of "showing plainly." It is a critical moment; for, whatever progress of doctrine the change may involve, all our satisfaction in its increased distinctness of outline and accumulated fulness of detail must depend on our assurance that *the teacher is still the same.* My next duty will therefore be that of noting the care which he himself has taken to fix that assurance on our minds. His care is never wanting where it is needed, and we have cause to praise his holy name that in this, as well as in so many other ways, he has knit together the one body of his written word by living and indissoluble bands, so that its interdependent parts fulfil effectually their several functions, in commencing or completing the one testimony of the great salvation.

It is of the testimony that I now speak. More happy is that common ministry in which we present the salvation itself. Only for the sake of the salvation does the testimony exist. There is a deep interest for every considerate mind in the form, the plan, the character, of the sacred writings; but it is not a merely literary or intellectual interest: it is one created by the object for which the writings are given. The reader of the Gospels is not suffered to close the volume without a solemn admonition of the purpose for which it has been placed in his hands. "These things are written that ye may believe that Jesus is the Son of God, and that believing ye may have life through his name." Does it wound our hearts to see this wondrous record misapprehended, its unity denied, its glory darkened? Perhaps it is a sadder sight in the eye of heaven when its inspiration is vindicated, its perfection appreciated, its majesty asserted, by one who at the same time for himself neglects the great salvation. Such a case is not impossible — perhaps is not uncommon. The Day will declare it. At least let it be remembered, that the study of the testimony is one thing, and the enjoyment of the salvation is another, and that the record of the things which Jesus did and said has attained its end with those only, who, " believing, have *life* through his name."

LECTURE IV.

THE ACTS OF THE APOSTLES.

THE FORMER TREATISE HAVE I MADE, O THEOPHILUS, OF ALL THAT JESUS BEGAN BOTH TO DO AND TO TEACH, UNTIL THE DAY IN WHICH HE WAS TAKEN UP, AFTER THAT HE THROUGH THE HOLY GHOST HAD GIVEN COMMANDMENTS UNTO THE APOSTLES WHOM HE HAD CHOSEN: TO WHOM ALSO HE SHEWED HIMSELF ALIVE AFTER HIS PASSION BY MANY INFALLIBLE PROOFS, BEING SEEN OF THEM FORTY DAYS, AND SPEAKING OF THE THINGS PERTAINING TO THE KINGDOM OF GOD: AND, BEING ASSEMBLED TOGETHER WITH THEM, COMMANDED THEM THAT THEY SHOULD NOT DEPART FROM JERUSALEM, BUT WAIT FOR THE PROMISE OF THE FATHER, WHICH, SAITH HE, YE HAVE HEARD OF ME.—*Acts i. 1-4.*

WITH these words we enter on a new stage of history and of doctrine, and they are words which connect it with the past. The links of Scripture (if I may so call them) uniting one part to another, and assisting our sense of the continuity of the whole, are worthy of especial notice. Thus the Gospels have been brought to a fit and (as it seems from the final words) an intended conclusion, at the end of the twentieth chapter of St. John; but yet another chapter is added, as if dictated by some afterthought, which in its effect links the whole Gospel record to the book which succeeds it. The miracle which had already foreshadowed the work of the fishers of men is repeated, but with altered circumstances, typical of the change which was at hand. For now the Lord is no longer with them in the ship, but stands dimly seen upon the shore; yet from thence issues his directions, and shows the presence of his power working with them in their seemingly lonely toil. Then the charge is left to "feed his sheep," and lastly the future destinies of the two chief Apostles are suffered to be faintly seen.

In like manner does the book of Acts at its opening attach itself to the preceding record; throwing back our thoughts on "the former treatise of all that Jesus began both to do and teach," and then passing rapidly in review the last circumstances which connect the Apostles with their Lord, as the instruments which he had chosen and prepared for the work which he had yet to do. Thus the history which follows is *linked* to, or (may I not rather say) *welded* with, the past; and the founding of the Church in the earth is presented as one continuous work, begun by the Lord in person, and perfected by the same Lord through the ministry of men. This is the point on which I have now to insist. "The former treatise" delivered to us, not all that Jesus did and taught, but "all that Jesus *began* both to do and teach, *until* the day when he was taken up." The following writings appear intended to give us, and do in fact profess to give us, that which Jesus *continued* to do and teach *after* the day in which he was taken up.[7]

There are then two points which claim our attention when we pass beyond that day, and enter on the second stage of New Testament doctrine. One is that *the authority is continued;* the other is that *the method is changed.* Our inquiries will naturally be directed (1) to the *evidence* for the first fact, and (3) to the *reasons* for the second.

I. First, then, I turn to the books which lie before us, to ask *what evidence they give, that the divine authority, which was self-evident in the first stage of teaching, is continued also in the second*, or, in other words, that this is as really as the other *a part of revelation*, and a period of divine communication of truth to man. The fundamental part of this evidence consists in the words, which were cited in the last lecture, from the mouth of the Lord himself: for in the words of *his* lips is centred the evidence for all teaching which he has given us through the lips of men. But we are now to see how these intimations are supported in the books which follow.

1. We find, then, that the doctrinal writings of the Apostles are prefaced by the book of Acts, some account of that which was done being given as an introduction to the record of that which was taught. The function of this book in the scheme of Scripture is of very high importance, in other respects, to which we must advert hereafter, and especially in that which concerns us now. *It is a record of the personal action of the Lord Jesus Christ in the first evolution of his gospel and formation of his Church.*

With him and with his last words on earth the book begins, reminding us of his commission and commands to the Apostles whom he had chosen. Then we see him depart, and they are left to their work. Yet they do not begin it till the promised Spirit is come; they wait for the promise of the Father, which they have heard of him. One transaction in the interval shows their own assurance that he who directed them so lately intends to direct them still: "Thou, Lord, which knowest the hearts of all men, show whether of these two thou hast chosen, that he may take part in this ministry and apostleship."[1] Such language intimates the relation in which they still felt themselves to their now unseen Master. But soon the promised gift is bestowed, and the dispensation of the Spirit has begun. And what in their view is the dispensation of the Spirit?

[1] Acts i. 24.

It is the agency and gift of Jesus. "Being by the right hand of God exalted, and having received of the Father the promise of the Holy Ghost, *he* hath shed forth this, which ye now see and hear."[1]

This view of the operation of the Spirit, as the medium through which the Lord Jesus wrought and taught, is carried through the whole course of the history which follows. As in the promise, so in the history, "*The Comforter* will come unto you" — "*I* will come unto you," — are but two sides of one and the same fact. On critical occasions and at each onward step the hand of the Master is made distinctly visible. The first martyr dies for a testimony, which is felt to be an advance on what had been given before, being understood to imply that "this Jesus of Nazareth shall destroy this place, and change the customs which Moses delivered us;" and his words are sealed by the vision of his Lord in glory. The consignment of the Gospel to the Ethiopian proselyte was another step in advance, and for this "the angel of the Lord spake unto Philip." The preaching of the word to Gentiles, and their admission into the Church, was a greater step; and for this the Lord intervenes by the mission of an angel to Cornelius, by a vision and a voice of the Spirit to Peter, and by a kind of second Pentecost to the converts themselves. But when the greatest step of all is to be taken in the onward course of the Gospel, then most visibly does the great Head of the Church make manifest his personal administration. A new Apostle appears; not like him who was added before Pentecost, completing the number of the original college, and losing his individuality in its ranks; but one standing apart

[1] Acts ii. 33.

and in advance, under whose hand both the doctrines and the destinies of the Gospel receive a development so extensive and so distinct that it seemed almost another Gospel to many who witnessed it, and to some who study it seems so still. How striking is the special authentication appropriated to this stage of teaching! This man's conversion, education, commission, direction, the Lord Jesus undertakes himself. Suddenly he meets him in the way, shines forth upon him in a light above the brightness of the sun, speaks to him by a voice from heaven, calls him by name, convinces, adopts, directs him, commands Ananias concerning him, and (apparently on repeated occasions) announces the use which he has decreed tc make of "the chosen vessel." The subsequent history is marked by continual testimonies of the same divine intervention, given at every step which might involve the doubt whether it were of Paul or of Christ. When his soul clave to the ministry among his own people, he was forced from it by immediate command: "It came to pass that, while I prayed in the Temple, I was in a trance, and saw him saying unto me, Make haste and get thee quickly out of Jerusalem, for they will not receive thy testimony concerning me: depart, for I will send thee far hence unto the Gentiles."[1] When he had fixed himself as a settled teacher in Antioch, "the Spirit said, Separate me Barnabas and Saul for the work whereunto I have called them." When he would have confined himself to the Eastern Continent, and turned, in his contemplated circuit, first to Asia, and then to Bithynia, "the Spirit suffered him not," and a divine message enabled him to "gather assuredly that the Lord had called him" to carry

[1] Acts xxii. 17, 18, 21.

his Gospel into Europe. Again, in Corinth, the Lord's own voice directed him to remain, as in the head-quarters of the Grecian world. In Jerusalem, when disheartened and perhaps doubtful of the course he had taken, his Master came to assure him of the acceptance of his past testimony, and announce the purpose that he should bear witness also at Rome; and finally in the shipwreck itself, when all hope of being saved was taken away, the declaration of the divine purpose was made yet more distinct: "Fear not, Paul, thou must be brought before Cæsar."

Thus does he, who at the commencement of the history was seen to pass into the heavens, continue to appear in person on the scene. His Apostles act, not only on his past commission, but under his present direction. He is not wholly concealed by the cloud which had received him out of their sight. Now his voice is heard; now his hand put forth; and now through a sudden rift the brightness of his presence shines. And these appearances, voices, and visions are not merely incidental favors; they are, as we have seen, apportioned to the moments when they are *wanted*, moments which determine the course which the Gospel takes, and in which a manifestation of divine guidance proves the divine guidance of the whole. The ship rushes on its way, shunning the breakers, dashing through the billows, certain of its track. The crew work it, but do not guide it. We can see the strong movements of the helm, and from time to time discern a firm hand which holds it. No chances, no winds or currents, bear it along at their will, but he who has launched it guides it, and he knows the course which it takes.

The divine direction, which is thus exhibited in the book of the Acts, is indeed the direction of a course of *action* rather than a course of *teaching.* It seems to be the guidance of the *movements* of the Gospel, rather than of the *formation* of the Gospel; and our present inquiry is concerned with the progress of its formation, not with the progress of its extension. Yet in the apostolic period these two kinds of progress co-exist, and, as it were, cohere; and the outward divine direction of the one is offered as surety for the inward divine direction of the other. In the earlier period, the things which Jesus began to *do* were the proof and support of the things which he began to *teach;* and in the later period, that which he continued to do, in the *acts* of his Apostles, is the pledge that in their *doctrine* also it was he who continued to teach. The inference is natural and is plainly intended, — *If the introductory historical book manifests the direction of the Lord in the acts of these men, then in the subsequent doctrinal books we must own his direction in their teaching.* Such an inference would be reasonable, if we regarded the teaching as simply an *accompaniment* of the acting; such an inference is inevitable, when we see that the delivery of the truth to the world is the one *end and object* of what is done.

I must further observe, that the facts recorded in the book of Acts are not only a pledge of the divine authority of the doctrine in the Epistles, but are also the *means* through which that doctrine was perfected. As the Gospel was guided through its conflict with the contemporaneous Judaism; as it spread from the Hebrews to the Grecians, to the dispersion, to the devout persons, to the heathen beyond; as it passed from Jerusalem to Antioch, to Corinth, to Rome; as it was presented to men first through Peter, and then through Paul, — its doctrines were gaining at every step in definiteness and fulness. Questions arose which compelled decision; new states of mind in receivers of truth called out, not new principles of truth, but new applications of it; and the growth of Churches and the advance of Christian life led to the settlement of points which could not have been raised till such a state of things had arisen. Under these circumstances, a divine guidance of events was only a means for the divine guidance of doctrine. If the Lord himself sensibly interfere, to send Peter to Cæsarea, and to call Paul to bear his name before Gentiles and kings, then not only those steps, but the doctrinal results of them, are visibly included in the purpose of God and marked with the seal of heaven.

More than this we can hardly ask for from the book of Acts, seeing that its province is in the outward scene, and its office is to record the march of events. We pass from it to the Epistles with the fullest assurance which such evidence can afford, that the doctrine which they contain is given by the Lord Jesus, and that, if it appear an advance upon that which he spake with his lips in the days of his flesh, that advance has been matured by himself.

In the Epistles which have for their province, not history but doctrine, some direct statements on this subject might perhaps be expected. Whether expected or not, they are certainly found. The great body of the Epistles are the writings of St. Paul. The change in the aspect of their doctrine as compared with the Gospel type bears chiefly the impress of his mind. It has been called, and may be properly called, the Pauline doctrine. Is it also absolutely the doctrine of Christ? or is it an individual variety of that doctrine, to be regarded (so far as it seems peculiar) as one allowable form of the original truth? a token that there shall be, a warrant that there may be, various systems of opinion in the Church? The question in fact is this, Is *the voice of Paul* speaking in the Scriptures to be taken by the Church as *the voice of Jesus?* This question has been answered by the history in the Acts. We have already recalled to our minds the special choice, and call, and commission, and direction, which were assigned to the Apostle born out of due time; the confirmation of his proceedings when they were most questioned, the divine fellowship in his course when it seemed most lonely. But there is yet a more direct answer than this; one which his own words supply.

In his writings in general he is careful to assert the reality of his apostleship, as conferred by immediate appointment and bearing the seal of God; and it is observable, that the strength of these expressions is proportioned to the occasions when the authority of the office involves the authority of the doctrine. In the Epistle to the Galatians, when he has to maintain *his* gospel as being *the* gospel, we find the precision which marks the language of one who knows what insinuations he has to negative: "Paul, an Apostle, not *of men*,[1] neither *by men*,[2] but *by*[3] *Jesus Christ*, and God the Father, who raised him from the dead." He declares himself to have been placed, not originally from men, nor mediately by any man's ministry, but by the very hand of Christ, in the chair from which his instructions are delivered, and thus he attaches the authority of the commission to the instructions which are given under it. But he goes farther, and affirms that those instructions themselves were no less immediately received from the Lord Jesus, than was the commission under which they were delivered.

[1] ἀπ' ἀνθρώπων. [2] δι' ἀνθρώπου. [3] διά.

Let me ask your attention to the language which this Apostle uses, when speaking of the sources whence the matter of his preaching was derived. Take first two passages from the First Epistle to the Corinthians. He says (ch. xi. 23–25), "*I have received of the Lord* that which also I delivered unto you, that the Lord Jesus in the night in which he was betrayed took bread; and having given thanks, he brake it, and said, Take, eat: this is my body, which is broken for you: this do in remembrance of me. Likewise also he took the cup, when he had supped, saying, This cup is the New Testament in my blood: this do ye, as oft as ye drink it, in remembrance of me." Again (ch. xv. 1–7), the same expression, though less full, is used in reference to another class of facts: "Brethren, I declare unto you the gospel which I preached unto you, which also ye have received. . . . For I delivered unto you first of all *that which I also received*, how that Christ died for our sins according to the Scriptures; and that he was buried, and that he rose again the third day according to the Scriptures; and that he was seen of Cephas, and then of the twelve; after that, he was seen of above five hundred brethren at once; . . . after that, he was seen of James; then of all the Apostles." Now place by the side of these statements two others, taken from the Epistles which follow. To the Galatians he says (ch. i. 2, 12), "I certify you, brethren, that the gospel which was preached of me is not after man; for *I neither received it of man*,[1] *neither was I taught it, but by revelation*[2] *of Jesus Christ;*" and to the Ephesians (iii. 2, 3) he speaks in the same strain, though with less emphatic precision: "Ye have

[1] παρὰ ἀνθρώπου παρέλαβον. [2] δι᾽ ἀποκαλύψεως.

heard of the dispensation of the grace of God, given to me to you-ward: how that *by revelation he made known* unto me the mystery."[1]

Between the first and the second of these pairs of texts a very remarkable difference appears. In the first, St. Paul seems to represent his own preaching as a link in the chain of tradition, "I received," "I delivered,"[2]: nor yet as the first link, for even the fuller expression, rendered "I received of the Lord,"[3] does not so fitly import an immediate communication, as a reception of that which had originated from the Lord, and was handed down by his commandment.(8) St. Paul, therefore, here appears to stand, in respect to the sources of his information, on the same footing as the Evangelist who was associated with him, and to speak of the facts of the manifestation of Christ, "even as they delivered them unto us,[4] who from the beginning were eye-witnesses and ministers of the word." On the other hand, in the second pair of statements, the contrary assertion is made, namely, that his gospel was not received from man, nor taught by man, but communicated immediately by revelation of the Lord Jesus.

The state of the case thus brought to light is in exact accordance with the view which is here taken of the manner in which the Lord perfected his word. The Gospel which the Apostles preached was a combination of historic facts with their spiritual interpretations; and the expression, "Gospel which I preached," is used by St. Paul in different places with more immediate reference to the one or the other of these elements. In the passages from the Epistle

1 κατὰ ἀποκάλυψιν ἐγνώρισέ μοι τὸ μυστήριον.

2 παρέλαβον, παρέδωκα.

3 ἀπὸ τοῦ κυρίου.

4 καθὼς παρέδοσαν ἡμῖν.

to the Corinthians he speaks of the first and fundamental part of his preaching, referring expressly to the publication of historic facts: — Christ died — he was buried — he rose again — he was seen of Cephas, &c. On the same night that he was betrayed he took bread — he gave thanks, and brake it — he said, Take, eat, &c.; and we learn that the Gospel, *as a body of historic fact*, was received by the Apostle Paul, as by all others who had not seen the Lord in the flesh, from those who were the appointed witnesses of his visible manifestation. In the two latter passages it is otherwise. Not the historic facts, but "the mystery" connected with them, is spoken of (in the address to the Ephesians) as the subject of the revelation received. And the Gospel of which he writes to the Galatians is plainly not thought of on its historical, but on its doctrinal side. The "other Gospel" into which the converts were "being removed" was not another account of the life of Jesus, but another set of inferences connected with it. When he went up to Jerusalem by revelation, and privately communicated to those of reputation "the Gospel which he preached among the Gentiles," we are sure that he laid before them, not the substance of the history which we read in St. Luke's narrative, but the substance of the doctrine which is embodied in his own Epistles. The whole argument to the Galatians turns upon the doctrinal element of the Gospel. It is of this, therefore, that he so solemnly affirms that he was not taught it by agency of man, but received it as direct revelation from the Lord; and this affirmation is made, not merely in respect of the general doctrine, but specifically of those parts of it which it was given to *him* to develop and defend: "the Gospel which was preached by me," — "*my Gospel*," as he elsewhere calls it, the Gospel under that particular aspect which he admits to be the subject of extensive doubt and complaint. The part in the progress of doctrine committed to St. Paul was to define, to settle, and to carry out to its practical consequences the principle of free justification in Christ, which (*as* a principle) was acknowledged and held before his voice was heard; and we learn from his own statements, that, for this special work, not only a special commission, but a special revelation was given him by the Lord Jesus, so as to clear and settle his own mind on those points on which he was sent to clear and settle the minds of others. In this way he was a minister and a witness, not of those things which he had heard from others, nor of those things which he had only thought out for himself, but of those things which his Lord had showed him in personal visits and distinct communications, according to the announcement made at the first commencement of this peculiar intercourse, "I have appeared unto thee for this purpose, to make thee a minister and a witness, both of those things which thou hast *seen*, and of those things in the which *I will appear* unto thee."[1] No! he was not only an inspired teacher adorned with the title of Apostle; he was an Apostle in the strictest sense of the word, a commissioned witness to others of direct communications of Jesus Christ to himself; one appointed to confirm to others the salvation which, in his own hearing, had begun to be spoken by the Lord.

The appearances and revelations vouchsafed to the Apostle of the Gentiles are thus conspicuously seen to connect themselves with the agency assigned to him in the

[1] **Acts xxvi. 16.** *ὧν τε εἶδες ὧν τε ὀφθήσομαί σοι.*

progress of doctrine; and the more carefully we examine his history and weigh his language, the more sensibly do we feel ourselves in the presence of that great fact, on the reality of which the faith of succeeding ages has reposed, namely, the continued personal administration of the Lord Jesus in founding his Church and perfecting his word.

This administration was manifested, as we have seen, by selection of agents, direction of events, angelic messages, visits in visions, special instructions, and distinct revela tions; yet these numerous interventions do not constitute the entire system of divine guidance, or even the chief part of it, but are rather to be regarded as additions to the normal method of administration which they serve both to assist and authenticate.

2. The normal guidance of the Apostles by their Lord was not occasional, but *habitual*, not through separate interventions, but *through the Holy Ghost dwelling in them*. So the promise ran that it should be; and so in fact it was.

The Day of Pentecost is the opening of the second period of the New Testament dispensation. It stands alone, as does the day which now we call Christmas: the one the birthday of the Lord, the other the birthday of his Church; the one proclaimed by praises sung by hosts in heaven, the other by praises uttered in the various tongues of earth. That change is significant: for now the Spirit conveys the true knowledge of the wonderful works of God into the recesses of the human heart. A dispensation is begun, in which the mind of God has entered into mysterious combination with the mind of man, and henceforth the revealing light shines, not from without, but from within.

"O God, who at this time didst teach the hearts of thy faithful people by the sending to them the light of thy Holy Spirit!" So speaks the Collect for Whitsunday; and, in so speaking, seizes at once the central idea of the event. That idea is often imperfectly apprehended: for in the dispensation of the Spirit there is so much that is visible on its surface, that our thoughts are apt to be arrested before they penetrate to its centre. Tongues and prophecies, and signs and wonders, gifts of the Holy Ghost dispensed according to his will, are visible results of the event, and they witness to the Gospel and clear its way. Below these superadded faculties, we are conscious of a mighty influence in the region of the emotions. We feel the presence of that comfort and strength, of that glow and fervor and joy, by which we see the men animated in the exercise of their new powers, and hear them speak with tongues and magnify God. But we must go further. The new powers seem as it were born from the new impulses; but whence do the new impulses proceed? Is there not a cause for these? Does the Holy Spirit limit his entrance into man to the region of emotion, which is but the surface of our nature, without reaching those inner springs from which, according to the laws of that nature, the emotions should themselves be quickened! No! be sure that the Holy Ghost has occupied the heart and centre of our being, and that, as the tongues are given as a vent for the fervor of emotion, so the fervor of emotion has its own origin in a sudden access of intellectual light. New apprehensions of truth, new views of things, which those thus visited had seen but had not understood, now burst in a moment on their minds, and from that moment continued to grow more distinct and more extended before their now enlightened eye. God at that time not only stirred, but *taught*, the hearts of his faithful people, and sent to them not only the warmth but "the *light*" of his Holy Spirit.

If this had not been so, what fulfilment would there have been of those promises of the Lord which we lately recalled to mind, respecting the nature and effect of the gift which was to follow his departure? He told his Apostles that they should "receive power," and he told them that they should receive "comfort," but we have seen that that on which he chiefly dwelt was the light of *knowledge* which should rise upon their minds. "In that day ye shall know;" "he shall bring all things to your remembrance;" "he shall teach you all things;" "he shall guide you into all truth;" "he shall receive of mine and shall show it unto you." These are plain assertions. It is enough that they were made by him who gave the gift, and certainly knew how to describe it. The rehearsal of these assertions belonged to the last stage of our inquiry; the evidence of their fulfilment is the thing before us now.

Those to whom these promises are given exhibit at the time a dimness of apprehension, a perplexity and disorder of thought, an incapacity to understand the things which they hear and see, which we, enlightened from the light which they afterwards obtained, most unreasonably count to be wonderful. It could not have been otherwise with the strongest and most penetrating intellects. But the fact of their condition of mind is undoubted, whether we ascribe it to personal deficiency or to the necessity of the case.

They were dealt with accordingly. From the moment when they saw their Lord ascend, they were in full possession of all the external facts of which they were appointed to bear witness. But they were not in possession of the spiritual meaning, relations, and consequences of those facts, and therefore the hour of their testimony was not come, and the interval was passed not in preaching but in prayer. As soon as the promise is fulfilled they lift up their voice and speak. Never were men so changed. Who does not note the accession of boldness, faithfulness, and fervor! But these are not separated and unsupported gifts. They manifestly have their origin in the certainty of assurance and intensity of conviction. The "boldness"[1] proceeds from "a full assurance;"[2] according as it is written "I believed and therefore have I spoken, these also believe and therefore speak." Their clear, firm testimony rises in a moment before the world, never hesitating or wavering, never to sink or change again, only manifesting more fully, as time advances, the largeness of its compass and the definiteness of its announcements. Ever after they speak as men would do who were conscious of a ground of certainty which could not be questioned, who could say that things "seemed good to the Holy Ghost and to them;"[3] that their word was "not the word of man but the word of God;"[4] that it was "the Spirit that bore witness;"[5] that they "preached the Gospel with the Holy Ghost sent down from heaven;"[6] that "things which eye had not seen nor ear heard, and which had not entered into the heart of man, had been revealed to them by the Spirit, which searcheth the deep things of God;" that they "had received, not the spirit which is of the world, but the Spirit which is of God, that they might know the things which are freely given of

[1] παρρησία.
[2] πληροφορία.
[3] Acts xv. 28.
[4] 1 Thess. ii. 13.
[5] 1 John v. 6.
[6] 1 Pet. i 12.

God;" that they "spoke these things, not in words which man's wisdom taught, but which the Holy Ghost taught;" and that they "could be judged of no man," because "none knew the mind of the Lord so as to instruct him, and they had the mind of Christ."[1] It is enough. The three testimonies concur — the testimony of him who gave the Spirit, the testimony of those who received it, and the testimony of the facts which ensued on its reception.

Are we then at a loss to know what was the nature of the gift which the Holy Spirit brought for the purposes of the apostolic work? Certainly it was vast and various — "a sevenfold gift;" but its most essential part lay not in tongues and powers which witnessed to the Gospel, not in the fervor and boldness which preached it, rather *it was the Gospel itself.*

The Gospel which the Apostles preached consisted of two elements, a testimony of external facts which fell within the region of the senses, and a testimony of the virtue of those facts in the predestined government of God, and of the consequences of them in the spiritual history of men, neither of which was it possible for the senses to certify. For the first testimony they needed but a clear and faithful memory. For the second also the same faculty would suffice, but only up to a certain point; namely, as far as they had received and understood the exposition of transcendental truth from the lips of the Lord Jesus. But we have seen that the salvation only began to be spoken by the Lord, and that he himself asserted that it would not be fully revealed by him, or understood by them, until the Spirit came. If the Spirit on his coming did not complete that revelation, then the

[1] 1 Cor. ii. 9-16.

Gospel which the Apostles preached must have been, in some of its most important features, partly a word of God and partly a word of man. Their witness of the death, and resurrection, and ascension of Jesus would demand an unqualified acceptance, but their representation of the sacrificial character and atoning merits of the death, of the life-giving power of the resurrection, and of the meditorial office in heaven, would be the result of their own inferences from the words which they had gleaned from their Lord; and, instead of being judged of no man, they would be judged of every man who could take a different view of the words which they repeated from that which they had taken themselves.(9) Thus the whole system of their doctrine would stand (like the image in the dream) on feet part of iron and part of clay, and would not wait long for the hour of its overthrow. But he who, in the face of all which has been now recalled to mind, should still treat their doctrine in this light, would plainly accuse of falsehood, not only the men, but their Lord himself; who, if he spoke true when he gave them the Spirit, led them thereby "into all the truth." The guarantees for this fact could hardly have been plainer or stronger than they are. We thank God that he has provided them, and we pass into the second stage of New Testament teaching with adequate assurances that he who before taught us on earth, now teaches us from heaven, and that we still "hear *him* and are taught in *him*."

II. We have not then changed our teacher, but *he has changed his method:* and I have now to point out *the reasons of the change*, by showing that it was fitted to conduct the advance of doctrine from the point at which it had then arrived.

It may be said that the change was simply a matter of

necessity, because he who had spoken with his lips was now to be received up into glory, and could no longer talk with his servants on earth. But though the change might be necessary, it was also "expedient" — expedient for *them*. So he represents it to his mourning and perplexed disciples, and adds the support of a strong asseveration. "Nevertheless I tell you the truth, it is good for you that I go away; for if I go not away the Comforter will not come unto you."[1] The change then takes place as an *advantage* to those who are subjected to it. For them a stage of revelation has come which demands a method of teaching more penetrating and internal than that which they had till then enjoyed.

It is in this character that the superiority of the later method consists, as is pointed out by the plain distinction, "He dwelleth *with* you, and shall be *in* you." Here are two methods appropriated to the two stages of New Testament teaching: and it is clear as day that the second is an advance upon the first. In the one, the teaching power is separated from, and external to, the mind which is being taught; in the other, it is interfused and commingled with it. The words, in the one, are divine announcements fitted to form the apprehensions of man; the words, in the other, are expressions of human apprehensions already formed under the divine agency. The teaching power has thus changed its method, in order to meet the exigencies of a more difficult stage of instruction.

The facts are finished when Jesus is glorified; the manifestation of the Son of God is perfect, the redemption is

[1] John xvi. 7.

accomplished, and the conditions of human salvation are complete.

The history must now be treated as a whole, of which the plan and purpose have become apparent. The time is come for the full interpretation of the facts, of their effects in the world of spirit, and of their results in human consciousness.

A doctrine then is needed, which shall sum up the whole bearing of the manifestation of Christ, which shall throw a full light on its spiritual effects, and which shall guide the minds of men in their application of it to themselves. Such a doctrine might be given from God in one of two ways: by voices from heaven, declaring what view men *ought* to take of the history which had passed before them, and what their faith and feelings *ought* to be concerning it; or by voices from men themselves, expressing the view which they *did* take, and the faith and feelings which were *actually* in their hearts. In the one case, we should have Apostles, who would be to us the messengers of God, *only* while they testified that they had received such and such revelations, and while they recited those revelations to us word for word; but all their other words would come to us on their own merits, as simply the words of holy and enlightened men. In the other case, we should have Apostles, whose representations of their own view of all which they had heard and seen, whose expositions of their own convictions and feelings, and of the processes of their own thoughts concerning the things of Christ, would be to us so many revelations from God of what *he intended* to be the result of the manifestation of his Son in human hearts.

Who does not see that this kind of teaching would exceed the other in completeness and effectiveness? It would be more complete; for we should thus have the word prosented to us in the final form which it was meant to take, that, namely, of *a word dwelling in us* — a divine announcement changed already into a human experience. It would be more effective; inasmuch as example is more so than precept, and the same voice, being to us both the voice of God and the voice of man, would affect our hearts with the double power of certainty and sympathy. Such a method of teaching could only be possible under some system of divine action which should fuse into one the thoughts of God and the thoughts of man; and this was effected by the gift of the Holy Ghost to the Apostles for the work whereto they were called.

I say *for the work whereto they were called*, for the same Spirit is diverse in operation, and divides to every man severally as he will. When the Church was anointed from above, the manifestation of the Spirit pervaded her whole frame, "like the precious ointment on the head, which ran down upon the beard, even upon Aaron's beard, and went down to the skirts of his garments." Even "on the servants and on the handmaids" did the Lord pour out of his Spirit, and the supernatural presence was disclosed in a vast scale of various gifts, ranging from that which was intense and supreme to that which was superficial and ancillary. But we speak now of that which was supreme. "*First Apostles.*" The ointment is poured first upon the head; and from thence the glittering drops descend upon the raiment. All the members have not the same office: — Are *all apostles?* No! the authorities, standards, and types of truth are so by direct commission, and the gift which they receive is one which makes them so indeed. As the office, so is the gift. An incommunicable office has an incommunicable gift. An office which is to be solitary and supreme in the Church forever has a gift adequate to secure the implicit confidence of long-descending ages.

Voices may be heard among us now which tend to impair that confidence; complaints of the distinctive use of the word "inspiration," as applied to the Scripture writers, assertions that "the Scriptures are before, and above all things, the voice of the congregation."

On what do these complaints and assertions rest? On the true conviction, that, in all the Church, and in all ages, there is the presence of the same Spirit. Yes! and on the false assumption, that the gifts of the Spirit are to all the same gifts. There is no principle in the Bible more clear, than that the gifts of the Spirit are diverse, and are, in character and proportion, adapted to the works which God assigns, and appropriated to the offices which he creates. Now it is certainly one thing to be a member, and another thing to be a founder, of the church. It is one thing to receive or to propagate the truth, and another to deliver it with the authority of God, and to certify it to the world forever.

The same clear view of the way of salvation, and of the unsearchable riches of Christ, which gladdened the soul of St. Paul, might gladden the soul of one who heard his words, and may now gladden the soul of one who reads them. For both there is the same Spirit and the same testimony; but the Spirit is given to the one, that he may originate that testimony; to the other, that he may receive it. There is a difference between being builded into the holy temple, which is the habitation of God through the Spirit, and being constituted a foundation, on which the future building is to rise at first and to rest forever. Such was the separate function of the Apostles of the Lord and

Saviour, a function which they shared with the special messengers of God who went before them, and even with their Lord himself. "Ye are built," said they to their brethren, — "Ye are built on the foundation of the Apostles and Prophets, Jesus Christ himself being the chief corner-stone."[1] The corner-stone is but part of the foundation, though it be the first and the chief part; and this consolidation of the corner-stone with the adjacent foundations, as one basement to sustain the building, exhibits in the plainest manner the fact, that the Church, *in respect of its faith*, rests upon a testimony which was delivered, partly by Jesus Christ in person, and partly by the agents whom for that purpose he ordained. Their inspiration as believers associates them with the whole Church; their inspiration as teachers unites them only with their Lord.

The consciousness of this position appears in the records of their preaching, and breathes through all their writings a lofty and unyielding authority. They speak as men having the Spirit to those to whom it is also given, yet as men empowered to deliver the truth which the others were only enabled to receive. St. Paul addresses himself to "those that are spiritual," but he shows them that it is *he*, and not they, who is "put in trust with the Gospel," and that the word which he utters is one to which they can add nothing, and in which they can change nothing. St. John exhorts those "who have an unction from the Holy One," but as having himself a kind of anointing in which they do not share, whereby he delivers the "message," and the "witness," and the "commandment," which they on their part recognize and accept. No! the voice that sounds

[1] Eph. ii. 20.

from these pages is not the voice of the congregation, but the voice of those who founded it by the will of God; and that character the congregation itself has asserted for the word in all ages. The written word has been the canon of the Church, because it was a voice which came *to* it, *not* because it was a voice which proceeded *from* it.[10]

To us at this day this word has come; and to us at this day the anointing from the Holy One flows down. For you, for me (thank God!) the teaching of the Spirit remains. It remains for the servants and the handmaids: and many an obscure and lowly brother in the streets around us can say for himself, as truly as St. Paul could say, "I have received the Spirit that is of God, that I may know the things which are freely given to me of God." But one who thus speaks can know that his convictions are really the teaching of the Spirit of God only in so far as they correspond with the eternal types of truth, which ascertain to us what the teaching of the Spirit is. Now, as in those apostolic days, he which is spiritual can show that he is so only "by acknowledging that the things which" those appointed teachers "wrote to us are the commandments of the Lord;" for the gift of the Holy Ghost to others is not a gift whereby they originate the knowledge of new truths, but a gift whereby they recognize and apprehend the old unchanging mystery, still receiving afresh the one revelation of Christ, ever approaching, never surpassing the comprehensive but immovable boundaries of the faith once delivered to the saints. This is the gift, the only gift, which we desire for our Church and for ourselves; for it is one which makes the written word a living word, which fills a Church with joy, and seals a soul for glory.

LECTURE V.

THE ACTS OF THE APOSTLES.

THEY CEASED NOT TO TEACH AND PREACH JESUS CHRIST.—*Acts* v. 42.

JESUS CHRIST is gone up into glory, and the Holy Ghost has come down into men: and we have seen that these events are represented to us, not as closing the course of revelation, but as opening a new stage of it. The questions which met us on the threshold have been answered, and we go forward with the full assurance that our first teacher is our teacher still, and that his second method of instruction is an advance upon the first.

We have now to ask, first, *What change appears in the aspect of the doctrine?* and then, *What is the plan on which it continues to advance?*

For a reply to these questions I address myself to that introductory book which gives us the external history of this part of the dispensation of truth. It is not the function of a historical record to work out expositions of doctrine, but such a book may be expected to present *the general character* which the doctrine bore, and to clear to our view *the agencies and the stages* by which it was matured. This is precisely what is done in the book of Acts. It is the purpose of the book to do it; a purpose which ought to be more fully recognized than it is.

There are works which are done with so natural and graceful a facility, that it seems to the superficial observer as if any one could have done them, or as if he who did them was only guided by casual impulse, while a more careful student will perceive that singular gifts were necessary to produce the results which seem so easy, and that a comprehensive design and an accurate judgment presided over arrangements which appear fortuitous. Such a work is the Acts of the Apostles. In a narrative all alive with graphic details, and written in a style of animated simplicity and natural ease, it carries us through a period of human history of incalculable interest and importance: one in which the effects of the manifestation of the Son of God were developed and tested; in which the life which he had introduced among men disclosed its nature and power, and the truth which he had left commenced its struggles and conquests; in which the Christian Church was constituted, gradually detached from its Jewish integuments, and brought to the consciousness of its freedom and catholicity; in which it verified its credentials, proved its arms, recognized its destinies, and commenced its victories; in which impulses were given which would never cease to vibrate and precedents were established to which distant ages would refer; in which solemn and exciting scenes, marvels and miracles, saintly and heroic characters, their labors, their conflicts, their sufferings, their journeyings, their collisions with all classes of men, seem to force upon the historian a confusing multiplicity of materials. Yet through all this he makes his way straight in one direction, as a man guided by that instinct of selection which belongs to the ruling presence of a definite purpose. It is just this definiteness of purpose which is apt to pass unobserved. It is nowhere announced, and the unconstrained freedom of manner and easy inartificial style suggest no thought of it. We seem sometimes to be reading a collection of anecdotes or personal memoirs of certain Apostles, and some critics have dealt with the book as if indeed it were but a chance collection of stories with which the author had happened to become acquainted, or as if a fragment of the acts of St. Peter had been prefixed to a journal of the travels of St. Paul.

But we know St. Luke's intelligent, inquiring mind, his opportunities of information, his "perfect understanding of all things from the very first," his personal intercourse with those "who from the beginning had been eye-witnesses and ministers of the word." We cannot for a moment suppose that his acquaintance with the "Acts of the Apostles" was limited to the facts recorded in the book; that he knew nothing of the proceedings of John or James, or of the manifold movements and events which were going on by the side of those which he has related. In fact, there is not a book upon earth in which the principle of intentional selection is more evident to a careful observer. There is indeed no reason *given* why one speech is reported and one event related at length, in preference to others which are passed over or slightly touched; yet when we reach the conclusion we see the reasons in the result. We find that by an undeviating course we have followed the development of the true idea of the Church of Christ, in its relations first to the Jewish system, out of which it emerges, and then to the great world, to which it opens itself. When the words and deeds of Philip or Stephen, of Peter or Paul, are implicated with this progress of things, we find ourselves in their company, but when we part from St. Peter without notice of his after-course, when we leave St. Paul abruptly at the commencement of his two years in Rome, we are given to understand that we have been reading, not their personal memoirs, but a higher history, which certain portions of their careers serve to embody or to illustrate. Even when the book is considered by itself, the unity and completeness of the result is plain; but when we look at it in its place in Scripture, observe its function there, and its relation to the books which follow, we see most clearly the definite purpose with which it places us and keeps us in that particular line of historical fact which involves the progress of doctrine.

It may be said that this is claiming too much; for that, whatever amount of design may be attributed to the author of the "Acts," we cannot ascribe to him the prophetic purpose of fitting his book to its present place in Scripture. No, certainly not to him; but the Church has ever held that another Mind presided over what was written in these pages, a Mind which purposed that we should have a Bible, and which, guiding the production of its component parts, has made it what it is.

I speak in accordance with this view of Scripture when I ask, What is the office which the book of Acts fulfils in the evolution of doctrine in the New Testament?

For a reply to this question I would point to three results which the book unquestionably yields.

1. It places in the clearest light *the divine authority* of the doctrine given during the period which it covers, as a doctrine delivered by those who, for that particular purpose, were filled with the Holy Ghost, and were agents of the personal administration of the Lord Jesus Christ. This, the first and most important part of the office of the book, has been considered in the last Lecture.

2. It represents *the general character* of the doctrine delivered by the Apostles to the world.

3. It traces *the steps of external history* through which the doctrine was matured.

These are the parts of its office on which I have now to dwell.

I. The *general character* of the doctrine as it appears in the Acts of the Apostles is presented in the words of the text, "They ceased not to teach and preach Jesus the Christ."[1] Similar expressions continually recur: "he preached Christ unto them;"[2] "he preached unto him Jesus;"[3] "he preached Christ in the synagogues;"[4] they "spake unto the Grecians preaching the Lord Jesus;"[5] "he preached unto them Jesus and the resurrection."[6] No such announcements as these are heard in the Gospels. The preaching spoken of there is not of the person but of *the kingdom*. Jesus comes "preaching the kingdom of God;"[7] "preaching the Gospel of the kingdom;"[8] and his parables and common teaching are not prominently about himself, but about "the kingdom of heaven." So also his disciples are sent out "to preach the kingdom of God," and are even charged to "tell no man that he was Jesus the Christ,"[9] and are forbidden to publish the manifestation of the fact "until the Son of Man be risen again from the dead."[10] And because of the absence of this personal proclamation by himself or his servants, we find John the Baptist troubled and perplexed, and sending a deputation of his followers in the hope of extracting such a public declaration; and the multitude at a later time complain

[1] *οὐκ ἐπαύοντο διδάσκοντες καὶ εὐαγγελιζόμενοι* Ἰησοῦν τὸν Χριστόν.

[2] Acts viii. 5. [3] Ibid. 35. [4] Ibid. ix. 20.

[5] Acts xi. 20. [6] Ibid. xvii. 18. [7] Luke ix. 2.

[8] Matt. iv. 23, and Mark i. 14. [9] Matt. xvi. 20.

[10] Matt. xvii. 9.

"How long dost thou make us to doubt? If thou be the Christ, tell us plainly;"[1] and the High Priest, at the very last, unable to obtain testimony to such a public claim, is compelled to resort to adjuration—"Art thou the Christ, the Son of the Blessed?"[2]

The change in the key-note of the preaching is very significant. Things had been tending towards it. The presentation of Christ to men had been going forward, and the scheme on which it is set before us in the Gospel collection marks the gradual manner in which the eye, looking for the kingdom, had come to be fixed upon the person. In the teaching of the first Gospel the idea of the kingdom, in that of the last the idea of the person, is predominant. In the Acts the two expressions are sometimes united, as when the Samaritans "believed Philip preaching the things concerning the kingdom of God and the name of the Lord Jesus:"[3] and yet again, with more evident purpose, in the end of the book, where Paul's exposition to the Jews at Rome stands as the last appeal to that people—"To whom he expounded, testifying the kingdom of God and persuading them concerning Jesus:" and yet again in the closing verse, which describes the two years' continuous ministry by the words "preaching the kingdom of God, and teaching those things which concern the Lord Jesus Christ."[4] Evidently

[1] John x. 24. [2] Mark xiv. 61. [3] Acts viii. 12.

[4] Acts xxviii. 23, 31. *Διαμαρτυρόμενος τὴν βασιλείαν τοῦ Θεοῦ, πείθων τε αὐτοὺς τὰ περὶ τοῦ Ἰησοῦ.* (ver 23.) *Κηρύσσων τὴν βασιλείαν τοῦ Θεοῦ, καὶ διδάσκων τὰ περὶ τοῦ Κυρίου Ἰησοῦ.* (ver. 31.) Compare this summary of the apostolic teaching at the end of the book with the summary of the last teaching of Jesus at its beginning: *δι' ἡμερῶν τεσσαράκοντα ὀπτανόμενος αὐτοῖς καὶ λέγων τὰ περὶ τῆς βασιλείας τοῦ Θεοῦ*

on purpose are the two expressions combined in this final summary, in order to show that the preaching of the kingdom and the preaching of Christ are one: that the original proclamation has not ceased, but that in Christ Jesus the thing proclaimed is no longer a vague and future hope, but a distinct and present fact. In the conjunction of these words the progress of doctrine appears. All is founded upon the old Jewish expectation of a kingdom of God; but it is now explained how that expectation is fulfilled in the person of Jesus; and the account of its realization consists in the unfolding of the truth concerning him, "the things concerning Jesus."[1] The manifestation of Christ being finished, the kingdom is already begun. Those who receive *him* enter into *it*. Having overcome the sharpness of death, he has opened the kingdom of heaven to all believers. Those, therefore, who were once to "tell no man that he was Christ," are now to make "all the house of Israel know assuredly that God hath made that same Jesus, whom they had crucified, both Lord and Christ;" yea, they are to proclaim that fact to every nation under heaven.

It is, I apprehend, by this change in the *character* of the preaching, that we are to explain the surprising difference in the *effect* of the preaching, as seen in the Gospels and in the Acts. For some three years, probably, did Jesus preach in the Temple, in synagogues, in houses, on the seashore, and by the wayside; yet it is obviously but a scanty band of professed believers whom he leaves upon the earth, and these too appear possessed but with a dubious and uncer-

"during forty days appearing to them and speaking the things *concerning the kingdom of God.*"

[1] τὰ περὶ τοῦ Ἰησοῦ.

tain faith. On occasion of an important gathering in Jerusalem, "the number of names together were about an hundred and twenty."[1] The largest number we ever hear of is that mentioned by St. Paul — "above five hundred brethren at once;"[2] and of these, according to St. Matthew, "some doubted."[3] But a few days later Peter lifts up his voice, and "the same day there were added unto them about three thousand souls."[4] And so the word grows and multiplies, till we hear of "a great company of priests obedient to the faith,"[5] and "many thousands[6] of Jews which believe;"[7] besides the suddenly-rising, rapidly-growing Churches in all parts of the Gentile world. Men have sometimes expressed their wonder at this difference in the effect of the Lord's own preaching and of that of his disciples; and they have been fain to ascribe it to the outpouring of the Spirit, which wrought a sudden change in the hearts of the hearers. But we have no encouragement to suppose that the three thousand who believed on the day of Pentecost received any *special* gift of the Spirit (such as originated on that day) until *after* they believed. This was promised by the Apostle as a gift, not preceding, but ensuing on their baptism. "Repent," said he, "and be baptized every one of you for the remission of sins, and ye shall receive the gift of the Holy Ghost." No! It is not on the hearers, but on the preachers that the mighty influence is said to have come. The true reason for the change in the effect of the doctrine is found in the change which had passed upon the doctrine itself, when "the Spirit of truth was come" to fulfil the prediction, "He shall glorify

[1] Acts i. 15. [2] 1 Cor. xv. 6. [3] Matt. xxviii. 17.
[4] Acts ii. 41. [5] Ibid. vi. 7. [6] Literally, myriads.
[7] Acts xxi. 20.

me." Christ was not preached before he suffered; after he was glorified he was. In the former period, he and his followers "preached the kingdom of God;" in the latter, "they ceased not to teach and preach Jesus Christ." Thus the great change in the effect of the preaching, which might seem at first sight to derogate from his glory, is, on further consideration, seen to enhance it. Only when it is possible freely and fully to publish the one "name under heaven given among men, whereby they must be saved," are their consciences thoroughly roused and their trust decisively secured. So has it been, and so shall it be in the Church forever. Oh, that the apostolic lesson may still have its fruit amongst ourselves! that our evangelists may still know where their power lies! and especially that it may be said of all who go forth to the work from this place, "They ceased not to teach and preach Jesus Christ!"

2. But now comes the question, What was this preaching of Christ? Some have paraphrased it as the preaching of his doctrine, of the holy lessons which he taught. Some, again, as the setting forth of his holy character, the beauty of his life, and the attraction of his love. But if this were the main idea of preaching Christ, then certainly the relative effect of his own teaching and of that of his disciples ought to have been just the reverse of what it was; for the actual hearing of the gracious words which proceeded out of his mouth, and the actual sight of his holiness and love, must be supposed more effectual than the mere account of them by others. Then Jesus Christ ought to have gathered the thousands and his disciples the hundreds; and the faith inspired in the first period ought to have been more decided and intense than that awakened in the second. But the contrary was the case. There was then something in the

later preaching which was not present in the earlier. Was it that the Messiahship of Jesus was then openly proclaimed, which men had before been left to infer from the things which they heard and saw? It was this — but more than this. Not only was the fact of the Messiahship proclaimed, but the nature of it was explained. The Christ who was now proclaimed was one who had died and risen again, and whom the heavens had received till the time of the restitution of all things. In these three facts the manifestation of the Son of God had culminated, and in them the true *character* of his mission had appeared. The old carnal thoughts of it had been left in his grave, and could never rise from it again. It was the "Prince of life" who had risen from the dead; it was the "King of glory" who had passed into the heavens. And no less did these facts declare the *spiritual consequences* of his manifestation; since they carried with them the implication of those three corresponding gifts, which we celebrate forevermore, saying with solemn joy, "I believe . . . the forgiveness of sins, the resurrection of the body, and the life everlasting."

Towards these topics the preaching of Christ in the Acts of the Apostles continually turns. Observe how the first and present blessing (the forgiveness of sins) is ever adduced, as the result of the wondrous history which the chosen witnesses rehearse. When they have told of the cross and passion, it is in this consequence flowing from it unto men that their sermons culminate and close. "Him hath God exalted to be a Prince and a Saviour, to give repentance to Israel and forgiveness of sins;"[1] "Repent and be baptized every one of you in the name of Jesus Christ,

[1] Acts v. 31.

for the remission of sins;"[1] "Repent ye therefore and be converted, that your sins may be blotted out;"[2] "Be it known unto you therefore, men and brethren, that through this man is preached unto you the forgiveness of sins; and by him all that believe are justified from all things from which ye could not be justified by the law of Moses;"[3] "To him give all the prophets witness, that through his name whosoever believeth on him shall receive remission of sins."[4]

Such is the burden of the apostolical preaching, as exhibited in the rapid sketches and brief summaries given in this book. It is a doctrine of "redemption by his blood, even the forgiveness of sins," conveying, through the simple act of faith, a present cleansing to the conscience, as the necessary qualification for the glory which is to follow.

Then, in the next place, that glory is shown to arise from the resurrection of Jesus, as the preparation for it does from his sufferings. I need not remind you of the "great power" with which, from one end of the book to the other, "the Apostles give witness of the resurrection of the Lord Jesus." Everywhere they preach a "Christ that died, *yea, rather*, that is risen again." This event is presented by them not simply as the seal of his teaching, or more generally (to use the poor and shrunken phrase of later times) as the proof of his divine mission, but as itself the cause and the commencement of that new world and eternal life which was consciously "the hope of Israel," and unconsciously the hope of man. Turn especially to the latter part of the book, and study the position taken by St. Paul in the last crisis of his controversy with the Jews. See how he falls

[1] Acts ii. 38.
[2] Ibid. iii. 19.
[3] Ibid. xiii. 38, 39.
[4] Ibid. x. 43.

back upon the *resurrection* of Christ as involving the realization of the hopes of his people and the fulfilment of all the promises of God. Some have treated as a mere expedient for his own deliverance at the moment that one voice which he cried in the Council, "Men and brethren, I am a Pharisee, the son of a Pharisee; *of the hope and resurrection of the dead I am called in question.*" But he needed no expedient, for he was then in Roman hands and under Roman protection. It was no pretence to serve a turn; it was the genuine language of his heart. In all his other speeches at this crisis the same idea reigns predominant. "I stand and am judged for the *hope of the promise* made of God unto our fathers: unto which promise our twelve tribes, instantly serving God day and night, hope to come: for *which hope's sake*, King Agrippa, I am accused of the Jews. Why is it judged by you a thing incredible *if God raises the dead?*" It is the self-same sound which we heard in the first discourse given us from his lips, when he cried to the Jews of the Pisidian Antioch, "Now we declare unto you glad tidings, how that the *promise* which was made unto the fathers, God hath *fulfilled* the same unto us their children, *in that he hath raised up Jesus again.*"

And when we read his mind upon this subject more fully in 1 Cor. xv., and indeed in the whole of his writings, we see how truly the resurrection of Christ did, in his view, include the realization of all the hopes with which the old covenant was pregnant; how entirely it was to him the *cause and actual commencement*, as well as the pledge and promise, of the resurrection and the life to man.

But I must not go further into this subject. I had only to indicate that the general character of the doctrine which appears in the Acts of the Apostles is an advance upon that delivered in the Gospels. I say that it is so, inasmuch as it does more than merely testify to the facts of the manifestation of Christ, as (to use an imperfect illustration) the summing up of a judge is an advance upon the evidence on which it is founded, since it adds to the rehearsal of that evidence the selection of its critical points, the representation of their force and bearing, and the intimation of the conclusions to which they lead. Thus does the preaching of the Apostles sum up the result of all that the Gospels have disclosed, by the direct preaching of Jesus to men's souls, and by preaching him especially as the Christ who has been perfected by death and resurrection; by death which provides for the present necessities of conscience in the forgiveness of sins, and by resurrection which provides for the longings and hopes of the soul in the life everlasting. The messengers of God in this book cease not to teach and preach Jesus the Christ, as a Saviour by these means and in this sense.

II. It is, however, the book not of the words, but of the acts of the Apostles, and we accordingly find in it the intimations rather than the expositions of doctrine. It assists our present inquiry in a manner more appropriate to its historical character, by laying down for us *the course of external events through which the doctrine was matured.*

I have already adverted to the systematic plan of the book, as following out this course of events with the instinct of an undeviating purpose. It carries us straight from the Gospels to the Epistles, as the span of some great bridge continues the road between dissevered regions. Take it away and what a chasm appears! "Paul, an Apostle of Jesus Christ, to saints that are in Rome, in Corinth, Thessalonica, Philippi, Galatia, Ephesus, Colossæ." Who is this

Paul, and in what sense is he an Apostle? We knew him not when the twelve were ordained. We saw him not among the witnesses of the resurrection. How came the Gospel to these places? and is it the same Gospel for these Gentiles as it was for the Jews? As for James, and Peter, and John, and Jude, we know and revere their commission: but we saw them last in partial ignorance and error, and we hardly know what the value of their words may be.

We have noted on a former occasion the answers to these questions which the book of Acts supplies — the anointing of the Holy Ghost qualifying the men to fulfil the commission which they had received, the guidance of Christ given to their steps and his attestations to their words and works, the call and commission of St. Paul and his special appointment to a special work, and the spread of the Gospel in the world, and the rise of the Gentile Churches. By means of this information we are brought to the point at which we can open the apostolic writings, first with a due sense of their divine authority, and then with a sufficient acquaintance with the persons, scenes, and facts with which they are connected, and (I may further add) with effective supports to our conviction of their genuineness and authenticity. But neither of these functions of the book is precisely that for which we now inquire. Between Gospels and Epistles there is need for a connection of a more internal kind. During the intervening time the doctrine was not only spreading, it was clearing and forming itself, or rather was being cleared and formed by the hand of its Divine Author. This was effected through a certain line of events and through the agency of particular persons. With these events and persons the Book of Acts is occupied.

It begins at Jerusalem, it ends at Rome. Between these

two points questions have been settled, principles carried out, and divinely implanted tendencies disclosed. Especially have the relations of the Gospel to Jew and Gentile been fixed forever. We see how all the story progressively ministers to this result.

First Peter presents the Gospel as the fulfilment of prophecy and completion of the covenant made with the fathers. Then the Hellenist element seems to eclipse the Hebrew, and Stephen rises to reason and to die. A large space is therefore given to the speech, which sets forth the progressive nature of the dealings of God with Israel, and shows the drift of that current of thought on which we are launched. The death of Stephen is not only an individual martyrdom, like that of James, so briefly mentioned afterwards; it is a great crisis, and stands as such in the narrative, with a clear intimation of the position which was assumed on the one side and rejected on the other. Straightway the Gospel spreads. First Hebrew, then Hellenist, by the ministry of Philip it soon becomes Samaritan, and at the next step by that of Peter goes in to men uncircumcised. In the story of Cornelius we have a detailed statement of the means by which the Lord manifested his will, that the Gentiles should hear the word and believe. Then we pass from the side of Peter to that of the new Apostle, to whom the carrying out of this principle is committed. Antioch becomes our starting-point, where the disciples are first called Christians. We follow the steps of the traveller, and see far and wide that God hath also to the Gentiles granted repentance unto life. Then an opposing power is felt within the Church, and Christian Judaism asserts that there is departure from the original scheme. The Council meets, and by testimonies of Scripture and of fact infers the verdict of God, and issues the high decision, "It seemed good to the Holy Ghost and to us." Then, and not till then, Europe is entered, and the great centres of Greek life are occupied; but still in every place does the Apostle address himself first to the Jews, and everywhere they reject and persecute him. Finally, he returns to the head-quarters of the nation, and presents himself there with every circumstance of conciliation, but claiming his place in the covenant and as a preacher of *the hope of Israel.* The scenes and speeches of that crisis are given with fulness, because they define the position of the Christianity which St. Paul represents towards the Jewish system, and its final and furious rejection by the Jewish people.[1] "Believing all things which are written in the Law and in the Prophets, and having committed nothing against the people or customs of his fathers,"[2] he and his creed are forced from their proper home. On it as well as him the Temple doors are shut. Lastly, before the Jews at Rome he closes the long struggle with the peroration furnished him by prophecy:—"Well spake the Holy Ghost by Esaias the prophet unto our fathers, saying, Go unto this people and say, Hearing ye shall hear, and shall not understand; and seeing ye shall see, and not perceive. For the heart of this people is waxed gross, and their ears are dull of hearing, and their eyes have they closed; lest they should see with their eyes, and hear with their ears, and understand with their

[1] Not, as some have put it, because Luke happened to be present. Rather, Luke was present because the scenes and speeches were to be reported.

[2] Acts xxiv. 14; xxviii. 17.

heart, and should be converted, and I should heal them. Be it known therefore unto you, that the salvation of God is sent unto the Gentiles, and that they will hear it."[1]

Now let no man think that the rejection of Jews and admission of Gentiles were the only result of this long history. Another result has been involved in it: Christianity itself has been finally drawn out of Judaism, the delicate and intricate relations of the two systems being dealt with in such a way, that (so to speak) the texture of living fibre has been lifted unimpaired out of its former covering, leaving behind only a residuum of what was temporary, preparatory, and carnal. In fact, the doctrine of the Gospel has been cleared and formed; cleared of the false element which the existing Judaism would have infused into it, and formed of the true elements which the old covenant had been intended to prepare for its use.

Two great principles, it seems to me, were fought for and secured, which may be expressed (though not with strict accuracy) by saying that *the Gospel is the substitute for the Law*, and that *the Gospel is the heir of the Law.*

a. In saying that *the Gospel is the substitute for the Law*, I do not mean that it is so, as doing what the Law had done before it came, nor yet as doing what the Law had been meant, but had failed, to do; but only as doing that which the Law had been *supposed* to do. The Gospel provides for individual souls the means of justification and the title to eternal life. This the Law had not done, had not been meant to do, and by Prophets and Psalmists had been asserted not to do. Yet it had sunk deep into the mind of those who were under it, that this was the very thing

[1] Acts xxviii. 25-28.

which it did. Scribes taught distinctly, and the people were possessed with the idea, that there had been a law given which could give life, and that righteousness was by that Law. Here was the conviction which had entwined itself with their patriotism and their religion. Here was their pride and boast, and the prerogative which severed them from all mankind. Then, as now, they looked for a Messiah, who was to perfect the keeping of the Law, and (in some sense) to save other nations by reducing them to its obedience, and (as appeared in the sequel) many received Jesus himself as the Messiah, without any material change in that idea. But when the death of Jesus was preached as procuring, and the resurrection of Jesus as originating eternal life, and when the simple act of faith in him was proclaimed as the means of sharing it, the antagonism of the two doctrines appeared.

It was first in the arguments of Stephen, and afterwards in the preaching of Paul, that this particular feature of the Christian system made itself felt in its bearing on the great Jewish error. Hence the passion, the virulence, and the rancor with which the two men were pursued. "This man ceaseth not to speak blasphemous words against this holy place and the law"[1] — so ran the accusation against the first martyr: and years afterwards the superintendent of his execution heard the same words shrieked out against himself, "Men of Israel, help! This is the man who teacheth all men everywhere against the people, and the law, and this place."[2] False aud odious allegations! Yet the doctrine of which the two men were the great exponents did really involve a flat contradiction of the prevailing

[1] Acts vi. 13.

[2] Ibid. xxi. 28.

Jewish *theory* about the people, and the law, and that place. Within the Christian Church the same theory held its ground, and in that quarter cost the Apostle a still closer and keener conflict, in order to vindicate and establish for Jew as well as Gentile the great principle, "By grace are ye saved through faith,"[1] or, as St. Peter expressed the same truth, "Through the grace of the Lord Jesus Christ we shall be saved, even as they."[2]

Still the anxious pastor in his parish, still the self-observant Christian in his own heart, learns how deep-seated and how stubborn is that principle in human nature, which seeks the starting-point of salvation in self rather than in God, in doing rather than in receiving, in work rather than in grace. By the common Jewish theory of the Law, that principle has fortified itself strongly, and clothed itself gloriously, with the usurped sanctions of God. The Judaizing doctrine would have perpetuated that usurpation in the Christian Church, and, in so doing, would have neutralized the Gospel itself. The keen eye of the selected champion saw in a moment the fatal consequences of customs turned into doctrines, which others, who believed as he did, were perhaps inclined to regard with indulgence, as signs of an affectionate veneration for ancient ordinances.

In his writings we see how his penetrating eye discerned the danger, and how his unsparing hand averted it: we see also that the intuitive discernment and the impulsive vigor were the result of a deep personal experience, both of the error which he resisted, and of the truth which he defended. In the Acts we are carried through the period of this con-

[1] Eph. ii. 8. [2] Acts xv.

test in the outward course of events, and when the history ceases in the hired house at Rome, the Gospel has fought itself free, and severed itself from Judaism, not merely in its form, but in its essence, proclaiming salvation by the grace of the Lord Jesus Christ, and *not* by the works of the Law.

b. The other principle which is contended for and secured is, that *the Gospel is the heir of the Law;* that it inherits what the Law had prepared. The Law, on its national and ceremonial side, had created a vast and closely-woven system of ideas. These were wrought out and exhibited by it in forms according to the flesh — an elect nation, a miraculous history, a special covenant, a worldly sanctuary, a perpetual service, an anointed priesthood, a ceremonial sanctity, a scheme of sacrifice and atonement, a purchased possession, a holy city, a throne of David, a destiny of dominion. Were these ideas to be lost, and the language which expressed them to be dropped, when the Gospel came? No! It was the heir of the Law. The Law had prepared these riches, and now bequeathed them to a successor able to unlock and to diffuse them. The Gospel claimed them all, and developed in them a value unknown before. It asserted itself as the proper and predestined continuation of the covenant made of God with the fathers, the real and only fulfilment of all which was typified and prophesied; presenting the same ideas, which had been before embodied in the narrow but distinct limits of carnal forms, in their spiritual, universal, and eternal character. The body of types according to the flesh died with Christ, and with Christ it rose again a body of antitypes according to the Spirit. Those who were after the flesh could not recognize its identity: those who were after the Spirit felt and proclaimed it. The change was as great, the identity was as real, as in that mystery of the resurrection of the body which the same preachers showed: in which the earthly frame must lay aside the flesh and blood which cannot inherit the kingdom of God, and must reappear, dead and raised again, another and yet the same, "sown in weakness and raised in power, sown in dishonor and raised in glory, sown a natural body and raised a spiritual body."

But I should speak amiss if I left it to appear that the Gospel inherited the ideas only of the preceding dispensation, and not, in one sense, their form also. Their written form it did inherit, unchanged and unchangeable. The Law and the Prophets, as scriptures, as a book, were still under the new dispensation what they had been under the old — the voice of the Spirit and the word of God. Nay! this written word belonged to the new dispensation more truly than to the old, for these scriptures also were now raised to newness of life, and were recognized as prepared for the uses to which they were now applied, and written less for the immediate than for the ulterior purposes, as St. Peter has expressed it, "Not unto themselves, but unto us they did minister the things which are now reported unto you by them that have preached the Gospel unto you with the Holy Ghost sent down from heaven."[1] This is ever the position of St. Paul, for, as one has truly said, "None of the Apostles has laid such stress upon the Holy Scripture as the Apostle of the Spirit and liberty."[2] And as this appears in his writings, so does it also in the his-

[1] 1 Peter i. 12.

[2] Baumgarten on the Acts, vol. iii. 78 (Clarke's Tr.).

tory. From his first reported speech at the Pisidian Antioch,[1] which bases all upon the Scriptures, still he goes on with the Scriptures in his hand, till he stands and is judged, "believing all things which are written in the Law and in the Prophets;"[2] and finally parts from the Roman Jews after "persuading them concerning Jesus, both out of the Law of Moses and out of the Prophets, from morning till evening."[3] This then is the position taken at the beginning and fought for to the end; and it is a striking sight to see how resolutely St. Paul insists that he and his doctrine are the true representatives of the Law and the Prophets, while he is being persecuted and cast out, as having betrayed and blasphemed them.

These two principles — what the Gospel does without the Law, and what the Gospel derives from the Law — do in fact contain the main substance of apostolic teaching. On the one side, the principle that men are "justified freely by God's grace through the redemption that is in Christ Jesus"[4] is laid as the deep foundation of all the various forms and applications of evangelical truth. On the other, the principle that the same things which were done under the old covenant in the region of the flesh are done under the new covenant in the region of the spirit, opens out into the doctrine of the mediatorial work of Christ in the true tabernacle, the sacrificial character of his death, the atoning virtue of his blood, the sanctification of believers as a kingdom of priests and an holy nation, and their destined inheritance in a promised land and a holy city of their God. The expansion of these doctrines

[1] Acts xv. 13, 41.
[2] Ibid. xxiv. 14.
[3] Acts xxviii. 23.
[4] Rom. iii. 24.

fills and forms all the Epistles, and each is distinctly wrought out by itself, the one in the Epistle to the Romans at the beginning, the other in the Epistle to the Hebrews at the end, of the course of the Pauline writings.

It is in the Epistles themselves that we behold this expansion and formation of doctrine. In the Book of Acts we are conversant rather with the providential circumstances through which the result was obtained. Great principles are wrought out and settled in men's minds only through some such process as is here disclosed; namely, by persons raised up to represent them, by consultations, reasonings, debates concerning them, by events which compel their more distinct assertion and test their hidden strength, and by the action of opposing principles, firmly resisted in their fierce assaults, or instinctively rejected in their subtle approaches. This, the common course of the development and establishment of all principles, is here presented to us as carried on under the manifested guidance of the Lord himself; who, by special interventions, raises up the persons, guides the events, and certifies the issues with his own signature and seal.

Blessing and praise be unto his holy name, because he has done this! For he has thus added to the manifestation of himself his own direction as to the way in which it is to be used. On what a sea of uncertainties we should else have been launched! Observe the vague and wavering doctrine which ensues whenever the divine attestation of the apostolical teaching meets with discredit or mistrust. Now the Gospel is nothing but a re-publication, pure and perfect, of the Law of God; now it is a proclamation of his universal fatherhood; now an exhibition of the beauty of holiness and the attraction of love; now the revelation of a righteous King and Head of the human race; now it seems little else than a negation, a sweeping away of all the ideas which a teaching supposed to be divine had fashioned through preceding ages. So it is when men proceed, as if the summing up of the manifestation of Christ had not been done for them, but was left for them to do. From all partial or perverted representations our refuge is with those who were actually commissioned to do it, and who, under a divine guidance adequate to the exigencies of that commission, ceased not to teach and preach Jesus Christ. Through the blessed ordinance of a written word they have not ceased to do so now. To us, even to us who are here alive this day, they preach him still; a Christ "who died for our sins and rose again for our justification;" a Christ who saves without the Law, yet one who is witnessed by the Law and the Prophets. So they preach, and so we believe. This was the beginning of the confidence and the rejoicing of the hope to the Church at its birth, and this beginning it will hold firm unto the end. It is for us to see that we bear our part in the long history of the faith, finding its reality in the joy of our own salvation, and transmitting its testimony to the generation to come.

LECTURE VI.

THE EPISTLES.

PAUL, A SERVANT OF JESUS CHRIST, CALLED TO BE AN APOSTLE, SEPARATED UNTO THE GOSPEL OF GOD . . . TO ALL THAT BE IN ROME, BELOVED OF GOD, CALLED TO BE SAINTS: GRACE TO YOU AND PEACE FROM GOD OUR FATHER, AND THE LORD JESUS CHRIST.—*Rom.* i. 1, 7.

THESE words are the beginning and end of the long superscription which opens the series of Apostolic Epistles. That superscription forms a close and living union with the preceding book, in which we have known Paul the servant of Jesus Christ, his calling to be an Apostle, his separation to the gospel of God, and have left him at its close testifying to that gospel in Rome itself. A still more intimate union will disclose itself to any one who studies the position which he takes up for his gospel and himself in the book of Acts, and then considers the succinct and explicit assertion of the same position in the intervening verses of this superscription, where he characterizes the gospel to which he was separated as that which "God had promised afore by his prophets in the Holy Scriptures, concerning his Son Jesus Christ our Lord, who was made of the seed of David according to the flesh; and declared to be the Son of God with power, according to the spirit of holiness, by the resurrection from the dead: by whom," he adds, "we have received grace and apostleship for obedience to the faith among all nations, for his name: among whom are ye also the called of Jesus Christ." Here the Apostle seems to stand before us as he did in the previous history, firmly holding his ground in the prophetic and historic line of the old covenant, and from that standing-point opening the dispensation of the Spirit, which has its source and its pledge in the resurrection, and claiming "all nations" for the "obedience of *faith*."

This witness of continuity is especially important in passing from the apostolic history to the apostolic writings, since the history gains significance from the doctrine, and the doctrine derives authority from the history. The persons and events in the Book of Acts are important because they were ordained for the working out of the truth of the Gospel. But *what* is that truth which they worked out?

Summaries of its general character occur in that book continually, and the points which are being cleared and established are strongly indicated; but we have *only* summaries and indications, and the sketches of doctrines presented to us are taken rather from without than from within. If we except the debate in the council of Jerusalem and the charge to the elders of Miletus, all the discourses reported in this book are addressed to those who are *not yet Christians.* So Christ was preached to the world: but how was he taught to the *Church?*

This element is wanting in the history: yet it is one which we should have naturally looked to find; and, as we are brought into contact with so many Churches, on whose incipient and unsettled Christianity the labor of St. Paul was spent, its absence is really remarkable. We are told how he passed two years at Ephesus, and a year and a half at Corinth, "teaching the word of God among them," how, revisiting his Churches, "he gave them much exhortation," and how he "was long preaching" in one assembly or an other of the brethren: but no particulars of these preachings, teachings, and exhortations are given: and, considering that we have specimens of every kind of address to those that are *without*, we might well ask why there is no example to show how men were taught *after they had believed.* But they who hold that the scheme of Scripture as a whole is of the Holy Ghost will not ask that question; for they see that this omission is part of a plan, which provides this information for us in a more worthy and perfect way; namely, by placing in our hands the collection of Apostolic Epistles.

These writings are addressed to those who are already Christians; as our text describes them, "called of Christ Jesus — beloved of God — called saints." Such high titles, repeated in the successive superscriptions, warn us that we are here in the esoteric circle of doctrine. Whatever progress of doctrine these writings exhibit, that fact is the key to it. It must be a distinctly *subjective* progress, working out the results of the manifestation of Christ in the consciousness of men.

Observe the point at which we have arrived, by the time that we finish the Book of Acts, and open the Epistle to the Romans. The facts of *the manifestation of Christ* have been completed, and have been testified in all fulness and certainty by the witnesses chosen of God. They have not only testified of the facts, they have summed them up; have announced their scope and purpose in the counsels of God, as effecting the redemption of the world, and have called men to partake in the fruits of that redemption by believing and being baptized. They have given this testimony, not as of themselves, but with *the Holy Ghost* sent down from heaven, whose witness is united with their own, and whose indwelling presence is given also to those who receive the testimony, in order to open its meaning and to seal its truth. Thus a *holy Church* is formed, which gradually proves itself *catholic*, and shows at once its power of expansion and its spirit of unity; and within its protecting framework there exists a *communion of saints*, a common participation in the same spiritual possessions by all whom a union with Christ has separated and sanctified to God; and thus men are joined to the Lord and united with each other, and rest in the consciousness that they have found the *forgiveness of sins*, the *resurrection of the body*, and the *life everlasting*. In its fundamental articles the Creed is now complete.

To this point the book of Acts conducts us, and at this point it leaves us.

It may be said, what more should follow? Christians exist. Christian communities are formed. Let them now be left to their ordinary and permanent resources.

So it might have been.—So in God's mercy it was not.

A new life had begun, intellectual, moral, and social, teeming with elements which could not but work and expand. It would have been hard to say with what force they would do so, or in what direction. *Now* the great ideas of the Gospel are old and familiar; and the very words which represent them have been sorely battered by controversy, and worn thin by use. But *then* the revelation of Christ had just broken, like an unexpected morning, on a weary and hopeless world. The stupendous events which had so lately passed on earth, the present actual relations with heaven which were witnessed to men by proofs within and around them, the prospect of things awful and glorious hastening on, and perhaps already near at hand, must have given a stimulus to thought and feeling, the first sensations of which it is not easy for us now to estimate. The Father revealed, the Son incarnate, the Holy Ghost sent down from heaven — redemption wrought, salvation given, the resurrection of the body, the eternal judgment, the second death, the life eternal — new principles of thought, new standards of character, new grounds of duty, new motives, new powers, new bonds between man and man, new forms of human society, new language for human lips — all coming at once upon men's minds, placed them, as it were, in a different world from that in which they had lived before. At the same time they carried into that world of thought all the tendencies, infirmities, and perversities of our nature, and revealed truth had to settle itself into lasting forms, to find its adequate expression, and to have its moral and social consequences deduced, under a variety of influences uncongenial to itself. So critical a period, on which the whole future of the Gospel hung, would seem to cry aloud for a continued action of the living word of God; such as might, with supreme authority, both judge and guide the thoughts of men, and translate the principles which they had received into life and practice.

The Lord recognized this necessity. He met it by the living voice of his Apostles; and their Epistles remain as the permanent record of this part of their work. They are the voice of the Spirit, speaking within the Church to those who are themselves within it, certifying to them the true interpretations and applications of the principles of thought and life which as believers in Jesus they have received. This is the function in the scheme of divine instruction which belongs to these writings; and I propose now to note some particular aspects in which their designation and adaptation to it will appear. Without entering yet into the examination of their actual doctrine, we shall see that the Epistles are fitted to form a course of teaching of the kind described, by their form, their method, their authorship, and their relative character.

I. The *form* in which this teaching is given to us is very significant. "The epistolary form," says Bengel, "is a preeminence of the Scriptures of the New Testament as compared with those of the Old."(11) It is a suggestive remark, reminding us of that open communication and equal participation of revealed truth, which is the prerogative of the later above the former dispensation; indicating too that the teacher and the taught are placed on one common level in the fellowship of truth. The Prophets delivered *oracles to the people*, but the Apostles wrote *letters to the brethren*, letters characterized by all that fulness of unreserved explanation, and that play of various feeling, which are proper to that form of intercourse. It is in its nature a more familiar communication, as between those who are, or should be, equals. That character may less obviously force upon us the sense, that the light which is thrown on all subjects is that of a divine inspiration; but this is only the natural effect of the greater fulness of that light; for so the moonbeams fix the eye upon themselves, as they burst through the rifts of rolling clouds, catching the edges of objects and falling on patches of the landscape; while, under the settled brightness of the universal and genial day, it is not so much the light that we think of, as the varied scene which it shows.

But the fact that the teaching of the Apostles is represented by their *letters*, is a peculiarity, not only in comparison with the teaching of the Prophets, but with ancient teaching in general, which is perpetuated either in regular treatises or in discourses or conversations preserved in writing. The form adopted in the New Testament combines the advantages of the treatise and the conversation. The letter may treat important subjects with accuracy and fulness, but it will do so in immediate connection with actual life. It is written to meet an occasion. It is addressed to particular states of mind. It breathes of the heart of the writer. It takes its aim from the exigencies and its tone from the feelings of the moment. In these respects it suits well with a period of instruction, in which the word of God is to be given to men, not so much in the way of information, as in the way of *education;* or, in other words, in which the truth is to be delivered, not abstractedly, but with a close relation to the condition of mind of its recipients.

Thus it is delivered in the Epistles. Christ has been received; Christian life has commenced; Christian communities have been formed; and men's minds have been at work on the great principles which they have embraced. Some of these principles in one place, and others of them in another, have been imperfectly grasped, or positively perverted, or practically misapplied, so as to call for explanation or correction; or else they have been both apprehended and applied so worthily, that the teacher, filled with joy and praise, feels able to open out the mysteries of God, as one speaking wisdom among them that are perfect. These conditions of mind were not individual accidents. Rome, Corinth, Galatia, Ephesus, supplied examples of different tendencies of the human mind in connection with the principles of the Gospel — tendencies which would ever recur, and on which it was requisite for the future guidance of the Church that the word of God should pronounce. It did pronounce in the most effectual way, by those letters which are addressed by the commissioners of Christ, not to possible but to actual cases, with that largeness of view which belongs to spectators at a certain distance from the scene, and with that closeness of application which personal acquaintance dictates and personal affection inspires.

Thus the fuller expositions of truth contained in the Epistles are based on what the first principles of the Gospel had already wrought in human hearts; and its doctrines are cleared and settled, developed and combined, in correspondence with the ascertained capacities and necessities of believers.

II. From the adaptation of the form I pass to that of the *method* which the apostolic writings employ in the completion of evangelical doctrine. The one is in perfect harmony with the other. It is a method of companionship rather than of dictation. The writer does not announce a succession of revelations, or arrest the inquiries which he encounters in men's hearts by the unanswerable formula, "Thus saith the Lord." He rouses, he animates, he goes along with the working of men's minds, by showing them the workings of his own. He utters his own convictions, he pours forth his own experience, he appeals to others to "judge what he says," and commends his words "to their conscience in the sight of God." He confutes by argument rather than by authority, deduces his conclusions by processes of reasoning, and establishes his points by interpretations and applications of the former Scriptures. Such a method necessarily creates a multitude of occasions for hesitation or objection, and it has been proposed to meet these difficulties by the principle, that we are bound to accept the conclusions as matter of revelation, but not to assent to the validity of the arguments or the applicability of the quotations. The more we enter into the spirit of the particular passages which have been thought to require that qualification, the more we feel that it can only have seemed necessary, from a want of real and deep harmony with the mind of Scripture. But I have no call to enter on that subject; my purpose is simply to draw attention to the fact, that not only in the conclusions given, but in the methods employed in reaching them, there is an outward guidance of the Christian mind and a visible purpose to provide such guidance.

Consider, for instance, the argument on justification in the early part of the Epistle to the Romans, which accomplishes every step by the aid of the former Scriptures. Why all this labor in proving what might have been decided by a simple announcement from one entrusted with the word of God? Would not the apostolic declaration that such a statement was error, and that such another was truth, have sufficed for the settlement of that particular question? Doubtless! but it would not have sufficed to train men's minds to that thoughtfulness whereby truth becomes their own, or to educate them to the living use of the Scriptures as the constituted guide of inquiry.

It is the same with those records of personal experience, and those effusions of personal feeling, which teach us how the revelation of Christ tells upon the believer's heart. We see, for instance, in the seventh and eighth chapters of the same Epistle, the writer's own heart thrown open; first in its passage from the law of sin and death to the law of the spirit of life in Christ Jesus; and then in the assured consciousness of the vast and various blessings, present and future, which belong to the children of God, and the heirs together with Christ, whom nothing shall be able to separate from the love of God which is in Christ Jesus their Lord. This is not only definite information, it is also effective education, showing the revelation of God as wrought into its ultimate and subjective form; and assisting by sympathy, and ratifying by example, the same processes in other hearts.

Yet we should speak amiss, if we represented the education of Christian thought as carried on in the Epistles only by methods which seem to place the Apostle on the same level with his readers. No! there is everywhere present, in the lofty and unwavering testimony, the sense of an authority which makes all things *sure;* and whenever occasions arise, as from Galatian perverseness or Corinthian disorder, it asserts its unhesitating and uncompromising claims. Again, when need so requires, there is a change in the common method; and the progress of doctrine is effected in the prophetic manner, by definite additions to former revelations: as when St. Paul informs the Thessalonians, "in the word of the Lord,"[1] of some particulars not before made known, as to the manner in which the dead and the living will meet the Lord at his appearing. Thus apostolical authority and direct revelation diffuse over the Epistles their certainty and their majesty; but yet the presence of these more commanding elements is not suffered to overpower that general character of doctrine, which is proper for those who are of full age, and who have themselves "an unction from the Holy One, that they may know all things."[2] The mind of the teacher still enters into a free companionship with the mind that is taught, so as to exercise and educate the spiritual faculties, at the same time conducting them with de-

[1] 1 Thess. iv. 13–17.

[2] 1 John ii. 20

cisive authority to conclusions which they might else have failed to reach.

III. Turn now to the *authorship* of these writings. If the form and method of this scheme of Christian education are important features of it, so also is the selection of its agents; for here, as in other departments of education, we may say that "the master is the school."

Who are the appointed teachers of the Church? Peter and John, the two chief Apostles; James and Jude, the brethren of the Lord. We take knowledge of them that they have been with Jesus, and own the highest authority which association with him can give. But the chief place in this system of teaching does not belong to any one of them, nor to all of them together. Their united writings form but a second volume, and that a very thin one, just one-fifth of the bulk of the first, to which moreover it bears in some degree a kind of supplementary relation. The office of working out the principles of Christian faith into full proportions and clearly defined forms was assigned to another, to "Paul, the servant of Jesus Christ, called to be an Apostle, separated unto the Gospel of God, which he had promised afore by his Prophets in his holy Scriptures."

Now is it not a remarkable and almost a startling fact, that this great office should have been assigned to one who had *not* been a witness of the Lord's life on earth, and had *nothing* to tell of things which he had seen with his eyes, and heard with his ears, and his hands had handled of the word of life? We remember the indispensable importance of this qualification for the original apostleship, as expressed on the appointment of Matthias: "Of these men which have companied with us all the time that the Lord Jesus went in and out among us, beginning from the baptism of John unto that same day in which he was taken up from us, must one be ordained to be a witness with us of his resurrection." Yet on him who had never companied with him, or even with them, for one single day, the most important, or, at least, the most extensive and enduring part of the apostolic work devolved. The peculiar qualifications, which in other respects fitted St. Paul for the work whereto he was called, have ever received a just appreciation and ample treatment. We can all perceive the active habit, the fervent spirit, the strong will, the warm affections, the tender sensibility, the exercised intellect, the subjective tendencies of thought, the vivid consciousness of his own inward history, the combination of Greek and Hebrew training, the thorough grounding of the mind in the Law and the Prophets, the profound experience of the false theory of Judaism, in its effects on his own heart, and in the practical consequences to which it once carried him; finally, the suddenness with which the Gospel came upon him, making him to know with a singular distinctness what is the contrast between salvation sought by law through works, and salvation found by grace through faith, and what is the change in the whole world within, when the law of the Spirit of life in Christ Jesus makes a man free from the law of sin and death.

Perhaps it is commonly felt that these qualifications outweighed the disadvantage at which he stood in comparison with the other Apostles who had been with Jesus, and that this accounts for the addition to their number of one in other respects specially fitted for the work, *although* born out of due time. But it will better consist with the principles on which his whole history must be judged, if we say, that his being born out of due time *was itself one of his qualifications.*

Now we must remember that it is the Lord, foreseeing and foreordaining all, who directs the course of these events. If, after choosing and training the Twelve, he calls another man, who has had no share in that training, and specially commits to him a department of the apostolic work, we cannot speak of such a step as an afterthought and supplement, as we might do if it occurred in some human undertaking, in which the original arrangements had proved inadequate. We may be sure that the call of St. Paul *after* the manifestation of Christ was finished, was as much a part of the divine plan, as was the call of the Twelve when that manifestation was beginning, and that the later call must have corresponded as truly with *his* appointed work as the earlier call did with *theirs.*

We are here led to the more distinct observation, that the apostolic testimony was twofold, — first to the *facts* of the manifestation of Christ, secondly to its intended *consequences* in the spiritual state of man.

It was necessary that those who were to represent the Lord to the world, in his words and deeds, his mind and life, should be men on whose hearts the holy image had been stamped by closest intercourse, and who could testify to others of what their eyes had seen. They who were so qualified did their work, and gave the knowledge of Jesus to mankind. Modern study traces the distinct outlines, and finds the solid fragment of their oral narratives deposited in the written Gospels. Still further, St. Luke's preface shows that these narratives were the regular instruments of Christian education, "the things wherein" catechumens "were instructed."[1] This kind of instruction has found its permanent form in the fourfold Gospel.

But believers were also to be trained to the full apprehension of the *effects* of the manifestation in their own spiritual life. The apostolic teaching on this subject is represented forever by the Epistles, and those documents are in a remarkable degree *restricted* to that particular office. We should naturally have expected in apostolic teaching an abundant reference to the words and acts of our Lord Jesus, as the prolific sources of instruction. But we do not find such reference, nor anything like it, till we come to the Epistles of James, Peter, and John, and catch again the sound of words which we had heard from their Master and ours. The great doctor of the Church had no such remembrances. His relations with the Lord only commenced after Jesus was glorified and the dispensation of the Spirit had begun. If the others were the Apostles of the manifestation of Christ, he was the Apostle of its *results;* and, in the fact of passing under *his* teaching, we have sufficient warning that we are advancing from the lessons which the life, and the character, and the words of Jesus gave, into the distinct exposition of the redemption, the reconciliation, the salvation which result from his appearing. In this way it was provided that the two correlative kinds of teaching, which the Church received at the first, should be left to the Church forever in the distinctness of their respective developments; for this distinctness of development in the second kind of teaching is both announced and secured by its being confided to St. Paul.

Yet a danger might arise; a danger which did attend

1 Λόγοι περὶ ὧν κατηχήθης. Luke 1. 4.

his living ministry, and which recent theories have been eager to revive. It might appear, that the Gospel which he preached was not so much a stage of progress as an individual variety, and that in following it out we had diverged from the track of the original doctrine, and were no longer sustained by the authority of the Twelve.

The Twelve, therefore, are joined with St. Paul, as authors together with him of the doctrinal canon of the Church, fulfilling this office through Peter and John, their natural leaders and original representatives, and in a more restricted measure through James and Jude, the brethren of the Lord, to the former of whom, in the second stage of the Church's history, so eminent and peculiar a position is assigned. Had we been permitted to choose our instructors from among "the glorious company," three of these names at least would have been uttered by every tongue; and besides our desire to be taught by their lips, we should, as disciples of St. Paul, have felt a natural anxiety to know whether "James, Cephas, and John, who seemed to be pillars," "added nothing to,"[1] and took nothing from, the substance of the doctrine which we had received through him. It was the will of God that this anxiety should be met. We have not been left to conjectures and surmises. We have words from these very Apostles, expressing the mind of their later life, words in which we recognize the mellow tone of age, the settled manner of an old experience, and the long habit of Christian thought. We not only meet the men whom we should wish to hear, but we meet them at the point where we should wish to hear them, now the venerated authorities in the Church which they had long

[1] Galatians ii. 9.

since founded, and fully cognizant of its intervening history.

Thus, if the collection of Epistles be intended to exhibit the fulness and maturity of Christian doctrine, the selection of its authors corresponds to the end in view; the man who is best fitted to conduct, being associated with the men who are best fitted to confirm, the exposition and development of the Gospel of Christ.

IV. In the last place I must advert, though it is only possible to do so very slightly, to the *relative characters* of the several Epistles, as complementary one to another, and constituent parts of one body of teaching.

1. The Pauline Epistles appear, with very small variation, to have been habitually ranged in that order in which we read them now; and it is one which on the whole, and in a certain measure, produces the effect of a course of doctrine. They fall naturally into groups, which stand, relatively to each other, in the places which they ought to occupy for purposes of progressive instruction. The Epistles to the Romans, Corinthians, and Galatians have a corrective and decisive character. They are the voice of the doctor of the Church, expounding with blended argument and authority the meaning and the bearing of the principles of the Gospel which his hearers had already received; so as to decide the uncertainties, and correct the divergences, which will always characterize every second stage in the history of truth. When the enjoyment of a new discovery passes into reflection upon it, and impressions begin to define themselves in words, and "good tidings" are shaping themselves into doctrines and laws of life, a time of danger and necessity has come. Then the vagueness and the incorrectness of many first impressions

come to light; then old habits of thought are found still to survive, and old principles return to enter into damaging or destructive combination with those by which they had seemingly been expelled. Then, through treacherous arts, through perverse moral tendencies, and even through logical weakness, the tender system of truth may suffer, in the period of its formation, injuries which will be forever fatal. The reader of the first three Epistles finds himself in the presence of such a state of things, and feels that the necessities, which are there met by the word of the Lord, would, if not thus provided for, have destroyed all security in any further advance of thought.

Especially in this point of view does the Epistle to the Romans claim the place which it has habitually held as the first step in the epistolary course. The subject on which it gives a full and decisive exposition is not only vital but fundamental; namely, the need, the nature, and the effects of the justification for individual souls which the Gospel preaches and which faith receives. As there can be no repose for a soul while that first point of personal anxiety, "How can man be just with God?" is left unsettled; so there can be no solidity for a system of doctrine till the true answer to that question has been distinctly shaped and firmly deposited. Moreover, if the Gospel of St. Matthew fitly opens the whole evangelical record by connecting it with the former Scriptures, so also for the same reason does this great Epistle fitly open the doctrinal series: for what the one does in respect of fact, the other does in respect of doctrine, justifying throughout the intimation with which it opens that the Gospel will here be treated as that "which God had promised before by his prophets in the Holy Scriptures." In the constant references, and in the whole line of argument, we see the illustrious genealogy and lineal descent of the Christian doctrine of justification by faith, traced, like that of Jesus himself, from Abraham and David, and vindicated by the witness of the Law and the Prophets; so that we enter on the final exposition of the truth with a settled sense that in all the successive stages of its revelation the truth has still been one.

In the Epistles to the Corinthians we have passed into another region of thought, conversing now among the Greeks who seek after wisdom. In the presence of a spirit of self-confident freedom, both in thought and conduct, or, in other words, in presence of the essential spirit of the world, rising again like a returning tide, the Gospel develops its divine and indefeasible authority, claims the subjection of the mind, and regulates the life of the Church.

In the Epistle to the Galatians it encounters, not the spirit of a presumptuous freedom, but the spirit of a wilful bondage, which returns after its own stubborn and insensate fashion to the elements of the world and of the flesh. In repelling this tendency, the apostolic doctrine asserts more strongly than ever its character as a revelation of Jesus Christ, and shines out more clearly as a dispensation of spirit and of liberty.

Thus in the first three Epistles the first questions have been answered and the first dangers averted; and the apostolic or Pauline doctrine has established its divine character[1] and developed its essential features.

[1] In the Romans, by connecting itself with the inspiration of the Old Testament; in the Corinthians and Galatians, by asserting its own (see especially 1 Cor. ii. and Gal. i.)

The following Epistles differ from this first group in the comparative absence of the controversial attitude and of the judicial tone. As those whose minds are now cleared, settled, and secured, we readily follow the Apostle to that more calm and lofty stage of thought on which he stands in his Epistles to the Ephesians and Colossians; when, no longer in collision with human error, he expatiates in the view of the eternal purposes of God, and of the ideal perfections of the Church in Christ. If inspiration was asserted in the other Epistles, here it is felt. We hear, not as before, the doctor of the Church expounding, confuting, and deciding, but rather a prophet of truth speaking as "one borne along by the Holy Ghost."[1] Yet in both Epistles this high strain passes by the most natural transition into the plainest counsels, and in the intervening Epistle to the Philippians the voice is not that of a prophet but of a friend.

Finally, the Thessalonian Epistles complete St. Paul's addresses to seven Churches, and, though first in the date of production, may fitly be read last in the permanent order, as being specially distinguished by the eschatological element, and sustaining the conflict of faith by the preaching of "that blessed hope" and "the glorious appearing and the coming of the day of God."[2]

To this body of doctrine the Pastoral Epistles add their suggestive words, on the principles and spirit of that office, which is at once a government to order the Church and a

[1] ὑπὸ πνεύματος ἁγίου φερόμενος. Who can read Eph. i. and ii. without being reminded of this expression of St. Peter, by the sustained swell and unbroken flow of the thoughts and language?

[2] A characteristic made very noticeable in the present division by chapters, each chapter in the first Epistle closing with the mention of this subject.

ministry to serve it; so that, in the acknowledged writings of St. Paul, we advance from the first momentous question of justification for individual souls, through a thousand various exigencies and unfoldings of the life of faith, till we reach the outer circle of ministerial provision for the care of the Church and the stewardship of the truth.

2. But, in passing through this course of teaching, we have been in continual contact with the reminiscences, the ideas, the imagery, and the language which are natural to one who was by origin and training a Hebrew of the Hebrews. With all his evangelical expansiveness of spirit, and all his antagonism to the false theory of the Jewish system, he yet has taught the things of Christ, and presented the universal salvation, under forms of speech and in a cast of thought which are derived from the school of the Law. Every moment it becomes a more serious question, whether this language is to be allowed for, as inaccurate in itself but under the circumstances of the case inevitable, or whether it is to be insisted on, as the method prepared in the purpose of God for the most adequate expression of spiritual truth. The question was indeed decided by the two facts, that the old covenant itself was a divine ordinance, and that its historical relations with the new covenant were a divine provision. Still it was of high importance to the clearness and fixedness of the doctrine, that this connection between the two covenants should be deliberately shown to consist, not in rhetorical illustration, but in a divinely intended system of analogies. This is the permanent office of the Epistle to the Hebrews, which, if not St. Paul's, is confessedly Pauline, and, apparently on account of its uncertified authorship, has usually taken its place in succession to his acknowledged writings. In its origin

it evidently belongs to the last hour of transition and decision, when a large number of men, who were at once Jews and Christians, stood perplexed, agitated, and almost distracted, as they seemed to feel the ground parting beneath their feet, and hardly knew whether to throw themselves back on that which was receding, or forward on that to which they were called to cling. In an intense sympathy with this perplexity, and even anguish, prevailing in the Hebrew-Christian mind, and in an intense anxiety as to its issue, the Epistle was written; a living voice of power in a time of change and fear, yet a comprehensive exposition of the advancing course of revelation, and of the relation between its two great stages. But more particularly is it to be noticed here, that this Epistle throws a stronger light than other writings had done upon the progress of doctrine during the Christian period itself. For, first, it expressly recognizes the fact that "the word of the beginning of Christ"[1] had been enlarged by intervening teaching into a "perfection," which many of those who are here addressed had sinfully and shamefully failed to receive; the teachers sent from God having wrought out for them full expositions of truth, to which their old prepossessions had closed their hearts. And, secondly, it exhibits the further fact, that this perfecting of the truth, by the full and definite interpretation of the principles of the Gospel, had been accomplished by means of the true reading of the Old Testament in the light of the knowledge of Christ.(12)

3. From the Pauline writings we pass to the collection of

[1] Heb. vi. 1. ἀφέντες τὸν τῆς ἀρχῆς τοῦ Χριστοῦ λόγον ἐπὶ τὴν τελειότητα φερώμεθα: "Leaving the word of the beginning of Christ, let us go on to perfection."

the Catholic Epistles. For all internal reasons they are better read in the place which they occupy in our Bibles than that in which the older manuscripts generally assign them, preceding the Epistles of St. Paul; for they are in effect the confirmation and the supplement of his doctrine.[1]

This character cannot here be proved, and it scarcely needs to be, for it is now in the main acknowledged. The personal characteristics of these writers are unlike those of St. Paul; the aspects of the truth are different, but the substance and the features are the same. Each writer, by the strongly distinguished lines of his own individuality, makes still more conspicuous the unity of the common faith.

The Epistle of St. James alone makes at first sight an opposite impression, and instead of harmonizing with the full development of evangelical doctrine, may appear to belong to an earlier, or rather a retrograde stage; and if taken as an intended exposition of the essential features of Christian truth, it might be thought to imply an Ebionite view of the Gospel, and even to betray an Ebionite origin. But the careful and candid student sees that the language employed distinctly presupposes the evangelical doctrine, and by supplementing other expositions of it does in fact acknowledge and confirm them.(13)

The harmony of the Epistles of St. Peter and St. John with the Pauline doctrine is sufficiently obvious, and the former Apostle not only practically (as is the case in an eminent degree), but pointedly and professedly sets his seal to the development which the Gospel had received in the teaching of the Apostle to the Gentiles, assuring those who had accepted the doctrine that "this is the true grace of

[1] See the latter part of Note I. In reference to this arrangement

God wherein ye stand;"[1] and again, instructing those to whom the "beloved brother Paul" had written "according to the wisdom given unto him," that they are to regard those writings as on a level with "the other Scriptures."[2]

On the Gospel doctrine itself, which is thus confirmed, a fresh light seems to be thrown by the spirit of these precious Epistles, the *faith* expounded by St. Paul kindling into fervent *hope* in the words of St. Peter, and expanding into sublime *love* in those of St. John. At the same time the reader cannot fail to note how these writings of the original Apostles, by express references, by borrowed language, and by their whole spirit, seem to bind the doctrine which the Epistles have developed to the Gospels in which it first began to be opened. Finally, he may observe with admiration the singular fitness of the few words of St. Jude to close the series of writings, through which the faith has been wrought out and consigned to the Church forever. It only remains for our last instructor to exhort us "earnestly to contend for *the faith once for all delivered to the saints;*" to warn us of the dangers of relapse; to entreat us "to build ourselves up on our holy faith, and praying in the Holy Ghost to keep ourselves in the love of God, looking for the mercy of our Lord Jesus Christ unto eternal life;" and, finally, to commend us "to him who is able to keep us from falling, and to present us faultless before the presence of his glory with exceeding joy."

With such charges, warnings, and commendatory prayers is the didactic portion of the New Testament left in our hands. We have now observed its function in the whole scheme of instruction, as addressed to those who have be-

[1] 1 Peter v. 12. [2] 2 Peter iii. 16.

lieved the Gospel, for the furtherance and perfecting of their education in Christ. We have seen that it is adapted to this work by the epistolary *form*, which contemplates those who are addressed as partakers in the same life with those who address them, and as brethren in the family of God. Secondly, by the *method* adopted, in which the teacher, putting forth all the varieties of his own mental energies, exercises and trains the spiritual faculties of those who are taught, while conducting them to definite and ascertained conclusions. Thirdly, by the appointment of the chief *author*, whose proper work only commences at the point where the testimony of the manifestation of Christ in the flesh is finished, and passes into the testimony of his present relations with men in the spirit. Lastly, by the *relative characters* of the collected writings, whereby the exigencies of the spiritual life are met at every point and provided for in natural though informal succession.

In concluding this survey I would sugest two questions which it may well leave upon our minds. First, What is our own experience of the exigencies thus provided for? The Gospel history accepted as true, some general statements concerning its consequences adopted, and a position in the Christian community assumed — these things seem to satisfy the minds of many among us. We see that the word of God does not contemplate so sudden and easy a satisfaction. It supposes that the believer in Jesus has entered on a vast world of life and thought. It supposes the existence of inquiries, anxieties, aspirations. It supposes a mind thoroughly aroused by the importance, the grandeur, and the glory of the truth which has come before it — a mind which purposes with itself "to apprehend the things for which also it is apprehended of Christ Jesus." It supposes the existence of hindrances difficulties, oppositions—things to be struggled through, as well as things to be striven after. What do you know of all this? Till you do know something of it, the Epistles are not for you. They are not written to suit a cool indifference, or to gratify a taste for discussion. The real condition for their use is the existence of that inward life for the necessities of which they provide. A man must turn the pages of the Epistle to the Romans with a sense of perplexity and distaste, if his own heart own no serious inquiry after the righteousness of God. The discovery in the Epistle to the Hebrews of all that is transacted within the veil, by the effectual ministry of the eternal Priest, can have for him but the slight interest which may attach to ingenious typology, if he feel no daily necessity to come himself to the throne of grace to obtain mercy and find grace to help in time of need; and the glorious standard of Christian character which every Epistle offers can but repel him, as something overstrained and inapplicable to actual life, if he have not recognized himself as bought with the precious blood and risen again with Christ. The whole scheme and course of teaching, meant for those who are "called to be saints," loses not only its force but its meaning for those who have no such project as those words imply.

The second question is this: If the exigencies which are thus supposed are really felt by us, what use do we make of the word which is given to meet them? We have seen that that word does not lead us to the entrance of the Christian life and then leave us at the threshold. It recognizes fully, it warmly enters into, all those anxious questions which arise in your hearts, as to the real nature of the work of Christ in which you are taught to trust, of that salvation which you desire to receive, of that life which you are called to lead, of those relations to God in which you are placed, of those great prospects which lie before you. And shall negligence or distrust deprive you of the assistance thus prepared, and leave you to encounter the thoughts which crowd upon the awakened soul, as if you had to deal with those only by means of your own resources? You are not so left. For those within the Church, those who have received Christ Jesus the Lord, those who own the holy calling, all this teaching is made ready. To them it is expressly addressed, and for their various necessities it is adapted. But it does not yield its true uses to a critical reference or an occasional consultation; only through a constant companionship and familiar intercourse does it tell effectually for its destined ends, and accomplish the blessed transformation of the poverty and vanity of this poor human life into the glory and reality of a life that is in Christ.

LECTURE VII.

THE EPISTLES.

OF HIM ARE YE IN CHRIST JESUS.—1 *Cor.* i. 30.

I TAKE this text, because it appears to me to contain the fundamental idea which underlies the whole range of the Epistles, and gives the specific character to their doctrine.

The specific character of their doctrine, as compared with the preceding parts of the New Testament, is the question which lies before me now.

Some kind of doctrinal progress must necessarily be attributed to these writings, if their words are taken as words of God; for everything in them which is not simple repetition must be in some sense addition, either giving information wholly new, or explaining, enlarging, and arranging that which former teachings had imparted.

It would therefore be fit, at the point which these Lectures have reached, to make some collection of these additions, or rather some selection of the chief instances of them; unless it should appear that this stage of the progress of doctrine is marked by such distinctive features, as suffice by themselves to describe the nature of the advance which has been made, and to supersede the accumulation of particulars by the peculiarity of a general character.

I. In what has been already advanced the existence of such a general character has been implied, and its nature has been in some degree defined.

We have looked upon the doctrine of the Gospels as the

manifestation of Christ to men, giving the conditions and the materials of a spiritual life which was to follow. We have looked upon the doctrine of the Acts of the Apostles, as the *preaching* of Christ to men, summing up the results of his appearing, proclaiming him with the witness of the Spirit, and gathering those who receive him into the form and the life of a Church. We have observed that the Epistles take up the line of teaching at this point, being a voice within that Church to those who are themselves within it; that they are appropriated by their superscriptions to those who are already called, separated, and sanctified in Christ; that they are marked by their form and method as instruments of education to the spiritual life after it has begun; and that the appointment of their chief author implies the purpose of teaching things which followed the completion of the work of Christ on earth, in his offices and ministrations in heaven, and in the dispensation of the Spirit amongst men. If the actual contents of the Epistles correspond with these intimations, their doctrine must necessarily bear a specific character as compared with that of the Gospels and the Acts. As the manifestation of Christ when it was finished made way for the preaching of Christ, so the preaching of Christ when it has been received opens into the *life in Christ*. The Epistles presuppose the existence of this life, both in the community and in the individual, and their doctrine is directed to educate and develop it. The fundamental thought in every page is that expressed in my text, "Of him are ye in Christ Jesus."

They are litle words, but they make an announcement of vast significance and boundless consequences. Writer and readers regard themselves and each other as having now entered on an existence, which for spiritual beings seems the only real one. "*Ye are*," says the Apostle. After speaking of "things that are not," and of "things that are," he turns to his fellow-believers, and says, "but ye are." And whence is this existence found? *From him*,[1] from God himself, as its immediate origin and still continuous author. And *where* is it found? "In Christ Jesus."

In Christ Jesus! As the simple voice of faith this word is ever uttered with joy unspeakable and full of glory. But preacher or commentator, who may attempt to sound the depths or open the treasures of its meaning, must feel his tongue falter under the sense of the inadequacy of every explaining word. Let us, however, at least assert the *reality* of the fact which it expresses, for it is no symbolical form of speech, but the statement of a fact, as real in regard to the spirit as the fact of our being in the world is real in regard to the body.

How does the vivid consciousness of this reality glow in the pages which are before us now! Christ has been manifested, preached, received; and what is the state which has ensued, as exhibited in the consciousness of those who have received them? They are not merely professors of his name, learners of his doctrine, followers of his example, sharers in his gifts. I may go further. They are not merely men ransomed by his death, or destined for his glory. These are all external kinds of connection, in which our separate life is related to his life only as one man's life may be related to another's by the effect of what he teaches, of what he gives, and of what he does. But it is assumed in the Epistles, that believers in

[1] ἐξ αὐτοῦ.

Jesus are no longer living a life that is only external, and, as it were, parallel to *his* life. They are *in* Christ Jesus, and he also is *in* them.

At the close of his manifestation he foretold a state of consciousness, which his disciples had not attained while he was with them in the flesh, but which would be enjoyed by them under the succeeding dispensation. "At that day ye shall know that I am in my Father, and ye in me, and I in you."[1] The language of the Epistles is the echo of this promise. It is the voice of those who have entered on the predicted knowledge, and who view all subjects in the light of it.

They know that *the Lord Jesus "is in the Father;"* or, as it is more fully and distinctly expressed by himself, that "*he is in the Father, and the Father in him;*"[2] not indeed with that character of knowledge which belongs to a later age, when abstract dogmatic statements were fashioned from their warm and living words, but rather with that kind of knowledge, to secure which to the Church forever those statements were needed and were framed. These writers know the truth, that the Father is in the Son, as constituting the power of the work of Christ on earth; and the truth that the Son is in the Father, as constituting the power of his mediation in heaven. On the one side, "*God was in Christ*, reconciling the world unto himself;"[3] on the other, it is "with *Christ in God*"[4] that the Christian's present life is hid.

Furthermore, these writers know that *believers are in Christ and Christ in them*, and show that knowledge, not

[1] John xiv. 20. [2] Ibid. x. 38; xiv. 10; and xvii. 21.
[3] 2 Cor. v. 19. [4] Col. iii. 3.

only by frequent assertions and a universal supposition of a close and vital union between the members and the head, but by a full development of both the aspects of this union, which the words of the Lord present.

Believers are in Christ, so as to be partakers in all that he does, and has, and is. They died with him, and rose with him, and live with him, and in him are seated in heavenly places. When the eye of God looks on them they are found in Christ, and there is no condemnation to those that are in him, and they are righteous in his righteousness, and loved with the love which rests on him, and are sons of God in his sonship, and heirs with him of his inheritance, and are soon to be glorified with him in his glory. And this standing which they have in Christ, and the present and future portion which it secures, are contemplated in eternal counsels, and predestined before the foundation of the world.

As the sense of this fact breathes in every page, so also does the sense of the correlative fact, that *Christ is in those who believe;* associating his own presence with their whole inward and outward life. They know that Jesus Christ is in them, except they be reprobates[1] (rejected ones). They live, yet not they, but Christ liveth in them,[2] and he[3] is their strength and their song.[4] This indwelling of Christ is by the Holy Ghost, so that the same passages speak interchangeably of the Spirit being in us, and of Christ being in us;[5] or of the Holy Ghost being in us, and our members being the members of Christ:[6] and so this word, "*I in you,*" includes the whole life of the Spirit in man, with all

[1] 2 Cor. xiii. 5. [2] Gal. ii. 20. [3] The ἐνδυνάμων Χρίστος.
[4] Phil. iv. 13. [5] Rom. viii. 9. 10. [6] 1 Cor. vi. 15. 19.

its discoveries, impulses, and achievements, its victory over the world, its conversation in heaven, and earnest of the final inheritance.

Thus, through the different but correlative relations represented by the words, "Ye in me, and I in you," human life is constituted *a life in Christ;* and, through the still higher mystery of the union of the Father and the Son, is thereby revealed as *a life in God.* "At that day ye shall know that I am in my Father, and ye in me, and I in you." Yes! as we pass through the Epistles, we see that that day is come, and that the consciousness thus predicted has been attained. It is no flight of mysterious rhetoric, but the brief expression of the settled, habitual, fundamental view of the state of those who are here addressed, "Of him are ye in Christ Jesus."

This idea underlies all that is said, gives the point of view from which every subject is regarded, and supplies the standard of character and the rules of conduct. We move in a new world of thought, and are raised to a level of doctrine which we had not reached before, though the Gospels had prepared us for it, and the Acts had led us towards it. In the Gospels we have stood like men who watch the rising of some great edifice, and who grow familiar with the outlines and the details of its exterior aspect. In the preaching of the Acts we have seen the doors thrown open, and joined the men who flock into it as their refuge and their home. In the Epistles we are actually within it, sheltered by its roof, encompassed by its walls; we pass, as it were, from chamber to chamber, beholding the extent of its internal arrangements and the abundance of all things provided for our use. We are here "*in* Christ Jesus." That is the account of the difference which we feel, and which lies in the opening out of the whole effect of the Gospel, rather than in additions made to its particular doctrines. The presence which was lately before our eyes, and drew us towards itself, now absorbs and wraps us round, and has become the ground on which we stand, the air which we breathe, the element in which we live and move and have our being.

The Churches are "in Christ;" the persons are "in Christ." They are "found in Christ" and "preserved in Christ." They are "saved" and "sanctified in Christ;" are "rooted, built up," and "made perfect in Christ." Their ways are "ways that be in Christ;" their conversation is "a good conversation" in Christ; their faith, hope, love, joy, their whole life is "in Christ." They think, they speak, they walk "in Christ." They labor and suffer, they sorrow and rejoice, they conquer and triumph "in the Lord." They receive each other and love each other "in the Lord." The fundamental relations, the primal duties of life, have been drawn within the same circle. "The man is not without the woman, nor the woman without the man in the Lord."[1] Wives submit themselves to their husbands "in the Lord;" children obey their parents "in the Lord." The broadest distinctions vanish in the common bond of this all-embracing relation. "As many as have been baptized into Christ have put on Christ; there is neither Greek nor Jew, there is neither bond nor free, there is neither male nor female; they are all one in Christ Jesus."[2] The influence of it extends over the whole field of action, and men "do all in the name of the Lord Jesus, giving thanks to God and the Father by him." The truth

[1] 1 Cor. xi. 11. [2] Gal. iii. 28.

which they hold is "the truth as it is in Jesus;" the will by which they guide themselves is "the will of God in Christ Jesus concerning them." Finally, this character of existence is not changed by that which changes all besides. Those who have entered on it depart, but they "die in the Lord," they "sleep in Jesus," they are "the dead in Christ;" and "when he shall appear," they will appear; and when he comes, "God shall bring them with him," and they shall "reign in life by one — Jesus Christ."

Pardon, my brethren, the necessarily slight and rapid manner in which you have now been reminded of this pervading characteristic of the Apostolic writings. Yet, swiftly as I am compelled to proceed, I must delay a moment; for there is a question which one who rehearses such words ought not to leave unspoken. What correspondence is there between our own habit of thought and the Christian consciousness which speaks in these pages? I mean, not in regard to particular doctrines or precepts, but in regard to that one fact which embraces them all — that which the text expresses, "Of him are ye in Christ Jesus." That is not the statement of a doctrine, but the summary of a life. Surely I must ask — Is it a life which I am living now? I glance over these pages, and see the holy and beloved name shining in every part of them, and mingling its presence with every thought and feeling, every purpose and hope. I see an ever-present consciousness of being in Christ, and a habit of viewing all things in him. Must I not look down into my heart, and ask whether my own inward life bears this character? Let me accept nothing in exchange for this. Men bid me live in duty and truth, in purity and love. They do well. But the Gospel does better; calling me to live in Christ, and to find in him the enjoyment of all that I would possess and the realization of all that I would become. In suggesting these personal inquiries, I have scarcely taken a step out of my way, for the very point before us is this, that the progress of doctrine in the Epistles is constituted, not in the first place by the communication of new information, but by the recognition of a spiritual state which has been attained, and by the education of the spiritual life pertaining to it.

II. It now remains for me to point out that this fundamental character does of itself constitute a visible advance in the *several parts* of doctrine, both changing their aspect, and enlarging their bounds; and for this purpose it is necessary to select some particular subjects in which this change may be studied.

1. We turn first to the primary doctrine of salvation by Jesus Christ. In the Gospels this doctrine appears in its most general form. To a great degree it is typically represented, through the bodily healing or saving which points to the like work in the world of spirit. On some occasions that faith, by which men are "made whole" or "saved" (as the word is variously rendered) in the lower sense, is declared to be the means of the higher blessing, and to have secured for the applicant "forgiveness of sins." To these intimations, definite invitations and assertions are added. He who speaks is "come to save the world;" "to seek and to save that which is lost;" men are called to "come to him that they may have life;" "he that believeth on him is not condemned;" "he shall never perish, but have everlasting life:" and from time to time some words are spoken which suggest the method in which the salvation is wrought—words which tell of "the Lamb of God who taketh away the sins of the world;" of

being "lifted up like the serpent in the wilderness," that those who look may live; of "life given as a ransom for many;" and of "the blood of a new covenant shed for the remission of sins." But, in reaching the Epistles, who is not struck with the definiteness and development which the whole doctrine, especially this last part of it, has obtained. Here men have already received the great truth in its first aspect, and have believed on the Lord Jesus for the remission of sins. Their minds, however, must work; and they search into the real depth and extent of the general assurances in which their souls at first found rest and joy. The word of God guides them through its commissioned interpreters. Thus the grounds of this salvation in the work of Christ, and the means of it in their own faith, are brought clearly and vividly into view, and the attention is fixed upon the *way* in which men, being sinful, are made the righteousness of God. In every variety of expression the reality of the atoning work of Christ is made sure; in every connection of thought it is made present. God "has set him forth to be a propitiation for sins through faith in his blood;"[1] "We are reconciled unto God by the death of his Son;"[2] "We are justified in his blood;"[3] "We have redemption through his blood, even the forgiveness of sins;"[4] we, "who were far off, are made nigh by the blood of Christ;"[5] "He hath made him to be sin for us who knew no sin, that we might be made the righteousness of God in him;"[6] "Christ hath redeemed us from the curse of the law, being made a curse for us;"[7] "By

[1] Rom. iii. 25. [2] Ibid. v. 10. [3] Ibid. v. 9.
[4] Eph. i. 7. [5] Ibid. ii. 13. [6] 2 Cor. v. 21.
[7] Gal. iii. 13.

his own blood he entered in once to the holy place, having obtained eternal redemption for us;"[1] "He was once offered to bear the sins of many;"[2] "He put away sin by the sacrifice of himself;"[3] "He bore our sins in his own body on the tree;"[4] "Ye are redeemed by the precious blood of Christ, as of a Lamb without blemish and without spot;"[5] "The blood of Jesus Christ his Son cleanseth us from all sin;"[6] "He is the propitiation for our sins, and not for ours only, but also for the sins of the whole world."[7]

Such is the constant voice of the apostolic teaching, and such also is the constant voice of that Christian consciousness which the apostolic teaching forms and certifies. Those who are in Christ are already inmates of that "holy temple" which we see reared in the Gospels and opened in the Acts; and for them the altar of the cross is the one central object, visible from the remotest precincts, and sanctifying all around it, while the one sacrifice thereon completed is the ever-present condition of all which is celebrated or enjoyed within. No mist invests the object to which all eyes are turned, such as may suggest or excuse the doubt whether that object be truly an altar, and the act accomplished on it a sacrifice indeed. Not here do we see believers "clinging (as it has been expressed) to the ground of fact" under the feeling that "mystery is the nearest approach that we can make to the truth; that only by indefiniteness can we avoid putting words in the place of things; that we know nothing of the objective act on God's part by which he reconciled the world to himself, the very description of it as an act

[1] Heb. ix. 12. [2] Ibid. ix. 28. [3] Ibid. ix. 26.
[4] 1 Peter ii. 24 [5] Ibid. i. 19. [6] 1 John i. 7.
[7] 1 John ii. 2.

being only a figure of speech; and that we seem to know that we never can know anything."[1] Instead of this we find a firm unsparing use of various but kindred forms of speech, each supplementing and confirming the other, and having in the minds of those who use them a recognized and settled force, derived from ordinances which they have always held to be divine, and which they now understand to have been pre-ordained for the very purpose of preparing the ideas and the language in which they are here expressing the things of Christ.

Mysteries of course remain; and the truths delivered, however distinct and clear in their central parts, have their circumference in regions which the eye cannot reach. I only observe that these central parts of the truth of our salvation become more distinct and clear as we advance beyond the threshold of the Gospel; and that in the Epistles, as standing amongst those who are in Christ, we receive a fuller interpretation of the things which he spake with his lips concerning the salvation which we were to find in him.

2. Proceed now to another doctrine respecting the Christian state — namely, that those who are saved are also sons.

One chief feature of the teaching in the Gospels is found in the word "Father." Jesus appears amongst men in the character of the Son. His first spoken word utters the consciousness of that relation, "Wist ye not that I must be among the things of my Father?"[2] His first introduction to men ratifies it: "This is my beloved Son in whom I am well pleased;"[3] and so he goes forth into the world as the Son of the Father. In right of this relation he straightway

[1] Jowett on the Epistles, vol. ii. p. 482.

[2] Luke ii. 49.

[3] Matt. iii. 27.

associates in it those who receive him: and when, in his first instructions, he lifts up his eyes on his disciples to teach them the principles of the kingdom of God, he bases everything upon this relation between them and their God. "Pray to thy Father;"[1] "Thy Father will reward;"[2] "Your Father knoweth what things ye have need of;"[3] "That ye may glorify your Father;"[4] "That ye may be the children of your Father which is in heaven;"[5] "Be ye perfect, as your Father which is in heaven is perfect."[6] So the whole course of his teaching tends to that intertwining of his own relation to God with theirs, which is finally expressed on the eve of his departure: "My Father and your Father, my God and your God."[7] And this language is not a mere general declaration of the universal fatherhood of God; for it is always addressed to his disciples *as such*, to the little flock whom the world will persecute, and to whom "it is their Father's good pleasure to give the kingdom:"[8] and it is further declared that the consciousness of it is only awakened in those who hear *his* word, for "no man knoweth the Father save the Son. and he to whomsoever the Son will reveal him;"[9] and the right to enjoy and feel this relation is represented by St. John as a gift to those who receive *him*, and believe in *him:* "To as many as received him, to them gave he power to become the sons of God, even to them that believe on his name: which were born, not of blood, nor of the will of the flesh, nor of the will of man, but of God."[10]

[1] Matt. vi. 6. [2] Ibid. 4. [3] Ibid. 8.
[4] Matt. v. 16. [5] Ibid. 45. [6] Ibid. 48.
[7] John xx. 17. [8] Luke xii. 32. [9] Matt. xi. 27.
[10] John i. 12.

What advance is made in the Epistles upon the doctrine thus announced? It appears there in a fuller *form*, and with plainer statements of its *ground* in the work of Christ, who is the Son sent forth, "made under the law to redeem[1] those who were under the law, in order that[2] we might receive the adoption of sons;"[3] and with stronger assertions of the *means*, on our part, through which the sonship is enjoyed. "Whosoever believeth that Jesus is the Christ is born of God;"[4] "Ye are all the children of God by faith in Christ Jesus."[5] But the substantive addition made to the doctrine lies in the region of *consciousness*, and in the experience of the inward life. Believers are in Christ, and so are sons of God, but, having become so, they find that Christ also is in them, giving them the *mind* of sons and the *sense* of their sonship. "Because ye are sons, God hath sent forth the Spirit of his Son into your hearts, crying, Abba, Father."[6] "The Spirit itself witnesseth with our spirit, that we are the children of God: and if children, then heirs; heirs of God, and joint-heirs with Christ."[7] This revelation is not only seen in the particular passages which assert it, but its presence is felt in all parts of the Apostolic writings, and as we read we become more and more sensible that Christ in the Spirit has perfected his teaching in the flesh, and that those who are in him have now learned all that was meant by his word "Your Father."

3. Turning now to the department of duties, let us take the first of them — the personal approach to God in worship, prayer, and praise.

[1] Buy out, ἐξαγοράσῃ. [2] ἵνα. [3] Gal. iv. 4.
[4] 1 John v. 1. [5] Gal. iii. 26. [6] Ibid. iv. 6.
[7] Rom. viii. 16, 17.

Speaking often on this subject, our Lord instructs us to come to God as a Father, and as one who seeth in secret;[1] to worship in spirit and in truth;[2] to pray always, and not to faint;[3] to pray as sinners who need mercy;[4] as children who are sure to be heard;[5] and whatsoever things we ask to believe that we receive them.[6] In his last discourse words are dropped, which seem to place the whole subject on a fresh basis: "No man cometh unto the Father *but by me;*" "If ye shall ask anything *in my name, I* will do it. Hitherto ye have asked nothing in my name: ask, and ye shall receive, that your joy may be full."[7]

In the Epistles these (at the time) anticipatory words have found their explanation; and thereby all the previous instruction is fully realized. Men are in Christ Jesus, and *therefore* they come to God by him. The whole character of worship and prayer is now derived from the consciousness that "through him we have access by one Spirit unto the Father."[8] God is approached as a Father indeed, because he is the Father of the Lord Jesus Christ in whom the worshipper is found: and therefore the two names are united in every voice and almost every mention of prayer. Through him also we have the access,[9] or, as it is soon afterwards expressed, "access with confidence by the faith of him."[10] The right of entrance is secured, and the means by which it was secured are present to the mind. We have "boldness to enter into the holiest by the blood of Jesus."[11] Sacrifice has been offered, the barriers are gone, a new and living way is opened. And yet, further, there is (as the

[1] Matt. vi. 8. [2] John iv. 24. [3] Luke xviii. 1.
[4] Luke xviii. 13. [5] Ibid. xi. 11–13. [6] Mark xi. 24.
[7] John xiv. 6, 14, and xvi. 23, 24. [8] Eph. ii. 18.
[9] τὴν προσαγωγήν. [10] Eph. iii. 12. [11] Heb. x. 19.

word implies) a present introduction by the living intervention of an eternal Priest, ministering in the true sanctuary, with active mediation and perpetual intercessions for all who come to God by him. Furthermore, this access, which is through the Son, is also "by one Spirit." To those who are in Christ the Holy Ghost is given, as the consequence of their union with him, and thus there is the Divine presence in the soul of the worshipper; and so, in the highest and most perfect sense, he worships the Father in spirit and in truth, and prays in the Holy Ghost, "the Spirit itself helping his infirmities, when he knows not what he should pray for as he ought, and making intercession for him with groanings that cannot be uttered."[1] Passing into the midst of such discoveries as these, we feel that the doctrine of prayer has attained its perfect form, by combination with the doctrine of the Trinity, and that the highest fulfilment of all which had been enjoined upon those who were *with* Jesus has become possible for those who now are *in* him.

4. The ethical teaching of the New Testament shall be my last example. There also the like kind of advance appears. I need not recall by any special references the characteristic features of our Lord's moral teaching in the Gospels. They are present to all our minds. That standard of character and rule of conduct have secured the reverential recognition of the common conscience of mankind and the genuine admiration of unbelief itself. It has been felt, even in unlikely quarters, that in those holy discourses and that perfect example, human character appears in a state of purity and elevation which is nowhere else to be seen: and especially that this moral system shines most

[1] Rom. viii. 26.

brightly in those points where other systems fail, namely, the truthfulness of inward cleansing, the majesty of lowliness, and the glory of love. Can there be advance on such a code as this, given by the Lord himself, when, as a man among men, he showed and taught what human perfection is?

Yet when we pass to the Epistles we are sensible of a momentous change. The standard is the same in its general elevation and in the proportions of its several parts. Where then is the change? I answer, in the *position* of those who are to use it, in the *relations* of which they are now conscious, and therefore in the *motives* by which they are to be influenced, and in the *powers* which they are supposed to possess. "Our duties," as Bishop Butler observes, "arise out of our relations."[1] Therefore every revelation of unknown relations must affect in some way the character of our duties. This truth comes strikingly into view as we follow the unfolding of the spiritual relations of believers to their Lord.

Observe first the position which the Lord Jesus attributes to those whom he teaches, and the consequent motives to which he appeals, in those instructions in righteousness which he gave in the days of his flesh. He urges the special relations in which those who have joined him stand. They are under peculiar obligations, and a peculiar government. They are *his* disciples,[2] and the children of their Father;[3] they must "do more than others."[4] He charges them as being their master, and counsels them as being their friend; and, as time goes on, uses the power of his example, and

[1] Analogy, Part II. chap. 1. sect. 2.
[2] Luke xiv. 26, 27, 43. [3] Matt. v. 45. [4] Ibid. 47.

at last appeals to the claims of his love: "I have given you an example, that ye should do as I have done to you;"[1] "As I have loved you, that ye love one another;"[2] then finally opens that deeper relation, from which their future fruitfulness must be derived: "Abide in me, and I in you. As the branch cannot bear fruit of itself except it abide in the vine, no more can ye except ye abide in me."[3]

That last saying, which was at the time a parable, they soon knew as a fact. When the redemption was completed, and he was gone from their side, they found themselves in a closer and deeper union with him than they had understood before. Henceforth it was in the relations with him, on which they had entered in the Spirit, that they found both the motives of duty and the power for its fulfilment.

The Epistles first unfold the fulness of the grace in Christ, and then beseech us "by the mercies of God" that we "present our bodies a living sacrifice, holy, acceptable unto God, which is our reasonable service."[4] They base their practical instructions on the consciousness of being redeemed with the precious blood of Christ,[5] of being risen with Christ,[6] of having the Spirit of Christ dwelling in us.[7] All goodness, righteousness, and truth are the fruit of the Spirit dwelling in us. We live in the Spirit, therefore we are to walk in the Spirit;"[8] we have received Christ Jesus the Lord, therefore we are to walk in him;[9] we are to flee fornication, because it would defile the members of Christ;[10] we are to put away corrupt communications because they will grieve the Holy Spirit of God, whereby we are sealed

[1] John xiii. 15. [2] Ibid. xv. 12. [3] Ibid. 4.
[4] Rom. xii. 1. [5] 1 Pet. i. 18. [6] Col. iii. 1.
[7] Rom. viii. 9, 13. [8] Gal. v. 22-25. [9] Col ii. 6.
[10] 1 Cor. vi. 19.

to the day of redemption;[1] we are to forgive one another, because God for Christ's sake has forgiven us;[2] to receive one another, because Christ received us to the glory of God;[3] and to give to others, because we know the grace of our Lord Jesus Christ, who, when he was rich, for our sakes became poor, that we through his poverty might be made rich;[4] our conversation is to be worthy of God, who has called us to his kingdom and glory;[5] we are to mortify our members upon the earth, because, when Christ, who is our life, shall appear, we also shall appear with him in glory.[6]

This character of ethical teaching is nowhere more conspicuous than in the calm depths of the Epistle of St. John, where the sense of fellowship with God is the ground of walking in the light;[7] and "he that saith he abideth in Christ ought himself also so to walk, even as he walked;"[8] and every man that hath the hope in Christ purifieth himself, even as he is pure;[9] and the love which laid down his life for us is the reason for a willingness to lay down our lives for the brethren;[10] and the whole spirit of love one to another is the reflection of that love of God, wherewith he first loved us, and sent his Son to be the propitiation for our sins."[11]

We recognize then the advance of ethical doctrine, not only or chiefly in its more various and detailed practical development, but in the fact that the principles, motives, and conduct of life are habitually drawn from the ever-present cousciousness of the great salvation. It is a habit of thought, up to which, but not into which, the moral

[1] Eph. iv. 29, 30. [2] Ibid. 32. [3] Rom. xv. 7.
[4] 2 Cor. viii. 9. [5] 1 Thess. ii. 11. [6] Col. iii. 4, 5.
[7] 1 John i. 6. [8] Ibid. ii. 6. [9] Ibid. iii. 2, 3.
[10] 1 John iii. 16. [11] Ibid. iv. 7-10.

teaching of Jesus had led us; a habit of thought, which corresponds with those relations towards himself, into which men fully entered only when his voice on earth had ceased. If there is this visible progress of doctrine in the department of Christian ethics; if, in respect of distinct exhibition of principles and motives, the teaching of the Apostles surpasses that of their Lord; it is plain that this fact is a necessity from the nature of the case. Till Jesus was glorified, his spiritual relations with believers could not be fully unfolded; and till those relations were apprehended, the motives arising out of them could not be called into action, nor the life resulting from them be clearly brought to light.

I have now adverted to some principal subjects on which we have received the teaching of God in the New Testament, as illustrations of the change which that teaching exhibits in the latter part of the volume. If we multiplied these examples to the utmost, our comparison of the aspect which every separate doctrine bears in the Gospels with that which it presents in the Epistles would still have the same result. We should still see that the later doctrine differs from the earlier, only as being its completion and fulfilment.[1] The Lord himself was perfected and glorified, not in the days of his flesh, but after they were ended. So also was his doctrine; but as in the later stage he is still the same Lord, so it is still the same doctrine. Its meaning is defined, its extent is disclosed, its consequences are deduced. Parable and proverb are changed into great plainness of speech. What seemed a figure is shown as a fact. What was intimation of something future is become

1 πλήρωσις.

assertion of something present. Motives are supplied, powers are assured, by which that which was enjoined is realized, and a life which had seemed impossible is now become simply natural. Revelation has only enlarged itself to meet necessities and fill capacities which its former words had purposely created. The earlier teaching contemplated the coming of a day for its disciples, in which many things should be said to them which they could not bear then. In the later teaching that day is come. At first they are taught as those who are *with* Jesus, afterwards as those who are *in* Christ. They know now that he is in the Father, and they in him, and he in them. When that consciousness is given, a standing-point is reached from which new worlds of thought may be surveyed. They *are* surveyed in the Epistles, and there the chosen teachers spread before us the unsearchable riches of Christ. They say to us, "Of him are ye in Christ Jesus;" and they show us what that state implies, of capacities, possessions, responsibilities, duties, and destinies; of relations to God and man, of connection with things in earth and things in heaven. They show that to produce and to perfect this state are the ends of the preaching of the word, of the institution of the sacraments, of the ordinance of the ministry, of the life and order of the Church; yea, of the divine government of the world, and of all that bears on human history. "All things are for your sakes;"[1] "All are yours, whether Paul, or Apollos, or Cephas, or the world, or life, or death, or things present, or things to come; all are yours; and ye are Christ's; and Christ is God's."[2]

[1] 2 Cor. iv. 15. [2] 1 Cor. iii. 21-23.

And so the great course of divine teaching has reached its highest stage. After slowly moving on, through the simple thoughts of patriarchal piety, through the system and covenant of the Law, and through the higher spirituality of the Prophets, it rose suddenly to a lofty elevation when God spake to us in his Son; and even higher yet when the Son ascended back into glory, and sent down the Holy Ghost to take up his unfinished word, and open the mysteries which had been hid from ages and generations. Each stage of progress based itself on the facts and instructions of that which went before. The Law was given to the children of Abraham, Isaac, and Jacob; the Prophets spake to those who were under the Law; Jesus Christ came to those who had been taught by the Prophets; the Holy Ghost instructed those who had received Christ.

Beyond, and outside this course of teaching, lay, and still lies, the great world of human beings. Lord, and what shall these men do? What is that to thee? *Follow thou me.*

Oh! let us follow. It is not the object of revelation to answer those inquiries, natural as they are. It *is* its object to lead *those to whom it comes* into that fulness of knowledge, and up to those heights of blessing, towards which, in its own historical progress, it so steadily advanced, and which its final stage attained.

Let not searchings of heart as to what others shall do, or the sense of the thousand questions which *must* wait for their solution a few years longer, divert us from now pressing into that inner circle of experience to which the Word of God conducts us.

There we shall find it true that "he that believeth on

the Son of God hath the witness *in himself*."[1] There we shall repeat within ourselves the words with which the last Apostle closes his Epistle: "We *know* that *the Son of God is come*, and hath given us an understanding, that *we may know him* that is true, and *we are in him* that is true, even in his Son, Jesus Christ. This is the true God, and eternal life."[2] There we shall feel that we have reached results for our own inward life answerable to all the preparations which went before — answerable even to the great facts in which those preparations culminated, when the Only-begotten of the Father came down to earth to take us into himself, and returned into glory to unite us to God.

[1] 1 John. v. 6. [2] Ibid. 20.

LECTURE VIII.

THE APOCALYPSE.

JOHN SAW THE HOLY CITY, NEW JERUSALEM, COMING DOWN FROM GOD OUT OF HEAVEN, PREPARED AS A BRIDE ADORNED FOR HER HUSBAND.—*Rev. xxi.* 2.

THESE words open the last vision of prophecy and the last teaching of Scripture.

It had been the promise of the Lord to his disciples that the Holy Ghost, whom he would send to them from the Father, should not only lead them into all the truth, but should also show them things to come: and we find the promise fulfilled in both its parts. The predictions of the great transitional discourse, concerning the coming dispensation of the Spirit, have their permanent justification in the canonical books which follow; and as the Epistles respond to the assurance, "He shall lead you into all the truth," so does the word, "He shall show you things to come," find its distinct fulfilment in the Apocalypse. That book continues the line of predictive history running through the New Testament, and is the consummation of the sure word of prophecy which pervades the Bible as a whole.

I have already had occasion to observe that the words spoken by our Lord in the flesh give the substance of all the later doctrine, and prove to be, as it were, the heads and summaries of chapters which were to be written afterwards. As all the great doctrinal features of the Epistles are found in germ in separate sayings of the Lord, so also the main outlines of the Apocalypse are given us in parables and sayings, which trace the future history of his kingdom. And more particularly it is to be noticed, that this book bears the same relation to the last discourse in St. Matthew, which the Epistles bear to the last discourse in St. John. In the upper room where the last Passover and the first Eucharist had been celebrated, and in the midst of the little company which then represented the Christian Church, the Lord spoke the words which opened the mystery of the spiritual life, a mystery afterwards to be fully unfolded by the Holy Ghost, in the day when they would know that he was in the Father, and they in him and he in them. Sitting on the Mount of Olives with Jerusalem spread before him, and questioned as to the sign of his coming and of the winding up of the age, he gave the outlines of a prophetic history, which contained the substance, bore the character, and must rule the interpretation, of the later and larger revelation.

Again, as in the case of the doctrinal teaching, so in the case of the prophetical, its unity is assured to us by the testimonies that the teacher is the same in the later as in the earlier stage. Not only do we find in the spoken words of the Lord the condensed substance of that which follows; not only do we hear from him, that this part of his teaching is to be continued by the Holy Ghost, whom he will send to show us things to come; but a peculiar care is taken in this last communication from heaven, to bring fully before the mind of the Church the reality of the presence of the Lord himself in his revealing word. "The revelation of Jesus Christ *which God gave unto him, to show unto his servants* the things which must come to pass," is a repetition, and a particular application, of that assurance on which all the Gospel rests, "*I have given unto them the words which thou gavest me.*" Even the visible discovery of this fact is not withheld. If Paul, as the great expositor of the present spiritual life, had seen Jesus Christ himself, and received immediately from the Lord that which he had delivered unto men; so John, as the prophet of the things to come, saw the well-remembered form again, surrounded with the symbols of majesty and judgment, and looked upon his countenance, now like the sun shining in his strength, and heard his voice as the sound of many waters.

Thus the continuity of the line of prophecy within the canonical books is made as clear as that of the line of doctrine; both commencing in the words of Jesus in the flesh, both perfected by the words of Jesus in the Spirit.

But it may be asked, If the line of prophecy is to be distinguished from the line of doctrine, what place can the former subject claim in Lectures which are appropriated to the latter?

Taking prophecy as predicted fact (however partially discovered or symbolically disguised), it will stand in the same relation to doctrine as is held by history or recorded fact. In the doctrine of the Gospel that relation is the very closest; for it is a doctrine which rests upon events. Its foundation is in facts which have come to pass, and will yet come to pass. Jesus died — he ascended — he will come again — he will reign in glory. These are external facts. They enter the region of doctrine (as we commonly use the term) through their consequences to ourselves, through their effect on our own inward consciousness, through the uses and applications which may be made of them. If Jesus died — to bear our sins; if he ascended — to be manifested in the presence of God for us; if he will come again — to judge our state; if he will reign in glory — to perfect our salvation; then these facts, in themselves external to us, are external no longer. They are among the grounds of a whole system of thought and habit of feeling, and, when taught as such, they grow into a scheme of doctrine. But as in history (I mean that which is commonly described as inspired history) all the events have not the same connection with doctrine, but some only an indirect and remote one, so also is it in prophecy; and particular facts, or a whole series of events, may be intimated in the way of prediction for other reasons, but not for any immediate bearing which they have upon doctrine.

It results from these observations that the progress of prophecy, taken as a whole, is so bound up with the progress of doctrine, that the enlargement of the one must in some degree involve the enlargement of the other. It also results that the one is still to be distinguished from the other, and therefore that it does not belong to such an inquiry as I now pursue to trace the details of a predicted course of events.

I am free then from all necessities of detailed apocalyptic interpretation; having only to render some account of the general doctrinal bearing of this revelation of things to come, and to point out what additions of that kind are made in the last book, to the treasures which the preceding documents have accumulated for our use. The separate accessions of information it would take long to gather, but their general character is visible at once.

I. The former Scriptures have revealed the Lord Jesus Christ as the Saviour, not only of individual souls, but also of "the body, the Church." The final result of his appearing is shown not only in the peace, the holiness, the participation and inherence in him of each separate person, but in the formation of a corporate existence, a society in which man is perfected, a kingdom in which God is glorified. The parables and sayings of the Gospels present this kingdom of God as having its own life and end, its own history and destiny, in which those of its individual members are involved. Soon its visible shape appears. A society is formed, and, if glorious things were spoken of the city of God under the old covenant, still more glorious things are spoken of this, which is "the house of God," "the Church of the living God,"[1] "the habitation of God through the Spirit."[2] It is not a mere aggregate of separate parts, but possesses an organic life, as "the body of Christ" "fitly joined together and compacted by that which every joint supplieth, according to the effectual working in the measure of every part, making increase of the body unto the edifying of itself in love."[3] It is endued with a corporate personality, in which the full results of redemption will appear: for it is the spouse of Christ, which he loved, and for which he gave himself, and which he will present unto himself a glorious Church, "not having spot or wrinkle, or any such thing."[4] In this view, the Church is not so much for the sake of the individual, as the individual for the sake of the Church. Its perfection and glory, its full response to the work of Christ, its realization of the purposes of God, constitute the end to which the existence of each member ministers. This line of

[1] 1 Tim. iii. 15. [2] Eph. ii. 22.
[3] Ibid. iv. 16. [4] Ibid. v. 27.

thought runs through the Epistles, and forms a distinct advance upon that which works out the development of personal salvation. I have now to point out that it is not perfected in the Epistles, but demands such a continuance and such a close as it receives in the Apocalypse.

The sense of sharing in a corporate existence, and in a history and destinies larger than those which belong to us as individuals, tends to throw the mind forward upon a course of things to come, through which this various history is to run, and these glorious destinies are to be reached. More especially is this the case, where there is a strong contrast between the ideal expectations which we have formed and the actual realization which at any particular time we behold. When present things in a measure disappoint us, we turn more eagerly to the brighter future, and look beyond the darkened foreground to the light which glows on the horizon. Who does not feel, in reading the Epistles, that some such sense of present disappointment grows upon him, and that such dark shadows are gathering on the scene?

How fair was the morning of the Church! how swift its progress! what expectations it would have been natural to form of the future history which had begun so well! Doubtless they were formed in many a sanguine heart: but they were clouded soon. It became evident that, when the first conflicts were passed, others would succeed; and that the long and weary war with the powers of darkness had only just begun. The wrestlings "against principalities and powers and the spiritual forces of wickedness in heavenly places"[1] were yet to be more painfully felt, and believers

[1] Eph. vi. 12.

were prepared to be "partakers of Christ's sufferings," and not to "think it strange concerning the fiery trial which was to try them, as though some strange thing happened to them."[1]

But worse for the Church than the fightings without were the fears within. Men who had long professed the Gospel "had need to be taught again what were the first principles of the oracles of God."[2] They were "falling from grace," and "turning back to weak and beggarly elements, whereto they desired again to be in bondage."[3] "Some had already turned aside after Satan,"[4] and, where there was no special prevalence of error, a coldness and worldliness of spirit drew forth the sad reflection, "All seek their own, not the things which are Jesus Christ's."[5] Contentions were rife, and schisms were spreading; and men, in the name of Christ and of truth, were "provoking one another, envying one another." New forms of error began to arise, from the combination of Christian ideas with the rudiments of the world and the vagaries of oriental philosophy. Here were men, like Jannes and Jambres who withstood Moses, "resisting the truth, reprobate concerning the faith."[6] Here were "Hymenæus and Philetus, who concerning the truth had erred, saying that the resurrection was past already."[7] Here was the "knowledge falsely so called,"[8] teeming with a thousand protean forms of falsehood. While the Apostles wrote, the actual state and the visible tendencies of things showed too plainly what Church history would be; and, at the same time, prophetic intimations made the prospect

[1] 1 Pet. iv. 12, 13. [2] Heb. v. 12. [3] Gal. iv. 9; v. 4.
[4] 1 Tim. v. 15. [5] Phil. ii. 21. [6] 2 Tim. iii. 8.
[7] 2 Tim. ii. 17. [8] 1 Tim. vi. 20. ψευδώνυμος γνῶσις.

still more dark: for "the Spirit spake expressly, that in the latter times men would depart from the faith, giving heed to seducing spirits and doctrines of devils,"[1]—that "in the last days grievous times should come," marked by a darkness of moral condition which it might have been expected that Gospel influences would have dispelled,[2]—that "there would be scoffers in the last days, walking after their own lusts, and saying, where is the promise of his coming?"[3]—that the day of the Lord would not be "till the apostacy had come first, and the man of sin had been revealed, the son of perdition, the adversary who exalts himself above all that is called God or an object of worship, so that he sits in the Temple of God, showing himself that he is God."[4] "The mystery of lawlessness was already working, and as antichrist should come, even then were there many antichrists,"[5] men "denying the Father and the Son," "denying the Lord that bought them,"[6] "turning the grace of God into lasciviousness,"[7] and "bringing on themselves swift destruction."

I know not how any man, in closing the Epistles, could expect to find the subsequent history of the Church essentially different from what it is. In those writings we seem, as it were, not to witness some passing storms which clear the air, but to feel the whole atmosphere charged with the elements of future tempest and death. Every moment the forces of evil show themselves more plainly. They are encountered, but not dissipated. Or, to change the figure, we see battles fought by the leaders of our band, but no secu-

[1] 1 Tim. iv. 1. [2] 2 Tim. iii. 1-5. [3] 2 Pet. iii. 3.
[4] 2 Thess. ii. 4-7. [5] 1 John ii. 18, 22. [6] 2 Pet. ii. 1.
[7] Jude 4.

rity is promised by their victories. New assaults are being prepared; new tactics will be tried; new enemies pour on; the distant hills are black with gathering multitudes, and the last exhortations of those who fall at their posts call on their successors to "endure hardness as good soldiers of Jesus Christ,"[1] and "earnestly to contend for the faith which was once delivered to the saints."[2]

The fact which I observe is not merely that these indications of the future are in the Epistles, but that they increase as we approach the close, and after the doctrines of the Gospel have been fully wrought out, and the fulness of personal salvation and the ideal character of the Church have been placed in the clearest light, the shadows gather and deepen on the external history. The last words of St. Paul in the second Epistle to Timothy, and those of St. Peter in his second Epistle, with the Epistles of St. John and St. Jude, breathe the language of a time in which the tendencies of that history had distinctly shown themselves; and in this respect these writings form a prelude and a passage to the Apocalypse.

Thus we arrive at this book with wants which it is meant to supply; we come to it as men who not only personally are in Christ, and who know what as individuals they have in him: but who also, as members of his body, share in a corporate life, in the perfection of which they are to be made perfect, and in the glory of which their Lord is to be glorified. For this perfection and glory we wait in vain, among the confusions of the world and the ever-active, ever-changing forms of evil. What is the meaning of this wild scene? what is to be its issue? and what prospect is there

[1] 2 Tim. ii. 3. [2] Jude 3.

of the realization of that which we desire? To such a state of mind as this, and to the wants which it involves, this last part of the teaching of God is addressed, in accordance with that system of progressive doctrine which I have endeavored to illustrate, wherein each stage of advance ensues in the way of natural sequence from the effect of that which preceded it.

Brethren, I would that this state of mind, these desires and wants, which the last revealing word supposes in those to whom it comes, did exist more extensively and distinctly among us. I think we must all feel that the piety of our day encloses itself too much within the limits of individual life.

That *I* should be pardoned, saved, and sanctified — that *I* should serve before God, and be accepted in my service — that *I* should die in peace and rest in Christ — that *I* should have confidence and not be ashamed before him at his coming — these are worthy desires for an immortal being, and for these the Gospel provides. But it provides for more than these; making me the member of a kingdom of Christ, and the citizen of a city of God. There ought surely to be a consciousness within me corresponding to that position; there ought to be affections which will associate me in spirit with that larger history, in which my own is included; and which will make me long that the kingdom of Christ should come, and the city of God be manifested. The blessedness ascribed to him that reads, and those who hear, the words of this prophecy, can belong only to those who read it and hear it thus.

II. Such being the state of mind which the book presupposes, and such the wants to which it is addressed, I have now to point out some leading characteristics of its doctrine in order to show what are the satisfactions which it provides. These characteristics, though distinguished from each other, will yet all be found to combine in one. The doctrine of the book is a doctrine of *consummation*.

1. It is a doctrine of the *cause* of the consummation. It educes the result from one source — the *atoning death* of Jesus. Is this an advance in doctrine? Has not the nature and efficacy of the great sacrifice been already sufficiently disclosed? Yes, certainly, in its bearing on personal salvation; but this book exhibits the connection between the personal and the general salvation, in the identity of their common cause. The personal salvation for each several soul has been expounded in the Epistles as found in Christ Jesus, and more particularly in our redemption to God by his blood. In these writings the sacrifice and propitiation of his death are ever before our eyes, as the cause of our restoration and the source of all our other blessings. When, in this book, we pass on from the personal to the general life, and are to see the victory secured, and the kingdom brought in, we may perhaps expect that the Lord will now appear only with ensigns and titles of majesty, as the conqueror and the king. It is not so. The opening doxology, "To him that loved us and *washed us from our sins in his own blood*," strikes the note of all which is to follow. When the historic vision begins, one is sought who may open the sealed purposes of God and conduct them to their end. "Then I beheld, and lo! in the midst of the throne, and the beasts, and the elders, stood . . . a *Lamb as it had been slain*,"[1] and his appearance wakens the

[1] v. 6–10. This passage is fundamental, as showing the *ground* of the power and the *means* of the victory, by the intentional contrast of images. ὁ λέων ἐνίκησεν . . . ἰδοὺ ἀρνίον ὡς ἐσφαγμένον,

song, "Thou art worthy to take the book, and to open the seals thereof: for thou wast slain, and hast redeemed us to God by thy blood out of every kindred, and tongue, and people, and nation; and hast made us unto our God kings and priests: and we shall reign on the earth." So the vision proceeds, and from the beginning to the end, through the long conflict, and in the midst of the glorious issue, there is still one title for him who conquers, and judges, and reigns. It is the Lamb who makes war and overcomes; and from the wrath of the Lamb kings and nations flee. It is the Lamb in whose blood his servants also overcome; in whose blood they have washed their robes; before whom they stand in white raiment; and to whom they ascribe salvation. In the Lamb's Book of Life the names of the saved are written. The Holy City is the bride, the Lamb's wife. The Lord God Almighty and the Lamb are the temple of it, and the light of it; and the river of the water of life flows forever from the throne of God and the Lamb. In the peculiar title, thus studiously employed, and illustrated by the repeated mention of the slaying and the blood, we read the doctrine, that the ground of the personal is the ground of the general salvation; that the place which the sacrifice of the death of Christ holds in the consciousness of the believer, is the same which it also occupies in the history of the Church, and that he conquers for us, and reigns among us, and achieves the restoration of all things, *because* he has first offered himself for us, and is the Lamb of God who takes away the sin of the world.

No view of the death of Jesus which fuses it with the rest of his example could have suggested the title by which this prophecy so persistently designates the conqueror and the king.

2. We have here, in the next place, a doctrine of the *history* of the consummation; I mean that besides a prophetic record of the facts of the history, we have (what is of much higher value) an exposition of the *nature* of the history. The book is a revelation of the connection between things that are seen and things that are not seen, between things on earth and things in heaven; a revelation which fuses both into one mighty drama, so that the movements of human action and the course of visible fact are half shrouded, half disclosed, amid the glory and the terror of the spiritual agencies at work around us, and of the eternal interests which we see involved. We are borne to the courts above, and the temple of God is opened in heaven, and we behold the events on earth as originating in what passes there. There seals are broken, trumpets are sounded, and vials are poured out, which rule the changes of the Church and of the nations. While we are looking down through the rolling mists on things that pass below, we are all the time before the throne of God and of the Lamb, and among the four and twenty elders, the four living beings, and the innumerable company of angels; and we hear voices proceeding out of the throne, the cries of disembodied spirits, and hallelujahs that roll through the universe. We see further, that there is cause for this participation of the world above in the events of the world below, for it becomes every moment more plain, that the earth is the battle-field of the kingdoms of light and darkness. There is a far bolder revelation than we have had before of the presence and action of the powers of evil. The old Serpent is on one side as the Lamb is on the other, and the same light which shows the movements of the Head and Redeemer of our race, falls also upon those of the enemy and

destroyer. In the sense of this connection between things seen and things not seen, lies the secret of that awe and elevation of mind which we felt as children when we first turned these pages; and the assurance of it has an ever-increasing value to him who has painfully sought to test the mingled forms of good and ill, and to discern some plan and purpose in the confused scene around him.

After noting the instruction given on the cause and the history of the great consummation, I come now to that which is given on its constituent parts, namely, the coming of the Lord, and the attendant facts of victory, judgment, and restoration.

3. The book is a doctrine of the power and *coming* of our Lord Jesus Christ. "Behold he cometh with clouds, and every eye shall see him."[1] That is the first voice, and the keynote of the whole. The Epistles to the seven Churches symbolical representatives of the whole Church in its various conditions) all take their tone from this thought, and are the voice of a Lord who will "come quickly." The visions which follow draw to the same end, and the last voices of the book respond to the first, and attest its subject and its purpose. "He which testifieth these things saith, Surely I come quickly. Amen. Even so come, Lord Jesus."[2] Whatever else the Christian desires is bound up in this prospect. The deliverance of the creation from its present groans and travail, the redemption of our body, the perfection of man in a holy community, and the realization in outward things of the tendencies of the renewed nature, all these hopes wait on the one hope of "*his* appearing." Towards that hope our eyes have been steadily directed in

[1] Rev. i. 7. [2] Ibid. xxii. 20.

the former apostolic writings; but it is here presented, not so much in relation to our personal life as to the kingdom of God and to the world itself upon the whole. It appears here as the "end of the world,"[1] towards which all things tend, and which the fuller manifestation of evil and the seeming victories of the enemy are themselves ordained to prepare. Differences and uncertainties of interpretation as to the details of this progressive history still leave us under the sense, that it is a history of the power and coming of our Lord Jesus Christ. This assurance, enjoyed at all times, grows clearer in the days of trouble, rebuke, and blasphemy, and the darkest times which the prophecy forebodes will be those in which its fullest uses will be found.

4. The doctrine of the coming is in itself a doctrine of *victory;* and that character pre-eminently belongs to the apocalyptic teaching. "In the world ye shall have tribulation, but be of good cheer, I have overcome the world." These were the last words of the Lord's last discourse; and ever after we feel their power in the actions, the bearing, and the words of his servants. They wrestle against the world, and principalities, and powers, but as men who are upon the conquering side, and who know that their Lord has already overcome these enemies, and triumphed over them in his cross. Therefore they also "are more than conquerors through him that loved them,"[2] and they record their conviction, that "whatsoever is born of God overcometh the world; and that this is the victory that overcometh the world, even our faith."[3] In the Apocalypse this spirit is still more distinctly felt; for there the virtual victory becomes a visible victory, both for the Lord and for his peo-

[1] συντελεία τοῦ αἰῶνος. [2] Rom. viii. 37. [3] 1 John v. 4.

ple. Every promise in the seven Epistles is addressed "to him that overcometh;" and the last Epistle unites the victory of the servant with the victory of the Lord: "To him that overcometh will I grant to sit with me on my throne; even as I also overcame, and am set down with my Father on his throne."[1] When the prophetic visions are to commence, the opening of the book is represented as the result of victory.[2] The first vision presents one who "goes forth conquering and to conquer;" and then, through all the changes of the conflict, we have the anticipations and presages of final victory. We are told of those who "overcome by the blood of the Lamb;"[3] we hear their shout of triumph, and see the palms in their hands; until in the last crisis the conquering armies of heaven sweep into sight, following the victor who has "on his vesture and on his thigh a name written, King of Kings and Lord of Lords."[4]

5. But victory for one side is overthrow and condemnation for the other; so that we have here also a doctrine of *judgment*. "The prince of this world is judged." That saying might stand as the summary of a large part of the book. He is judged — judged *as* the prince of this world — and this world is involved in his judgment. The reality of some possession of this world by the power of evil, and the

[1] Rev. iii. 21.

[2] Rev. v. 5. ἰδοὺ ἐνίκησεν ὁ λέων ὁ ὢν ἐκ τῆς φυλῆς Ἰούδα ἀνοῖξαι τὸ βιβλίον. "Behold the Lion of the tribe of Judah prevailed to open the book." The variety of the words employed in the Authorized Version (overcome, prevail, conquer, victory) to represent the one word in the Greek, has the effect of diminishing the impression which this feature in the language would otherwise make on the reader.

[3] Rev. xii. 11. [4] Ibid. xix. 11-16.

certainty of its judicial consequences to him and to it, had been revealed with increasing distinctness through the former writings; till in two of the last Epistles the "terrible voice of most just judgment" had swelled into the full tones, to which our ears had been accustomed in Old Testament prophecy. I need not recall by particular citations the manner in which this line of teaching is carried out in the Apocalypse, the various forms of strong development in which the power of evil is represented as appearing, or the plagues, and punishment, and final overthrow, which are its portion from the Lord. The opening proclamation of the coming notifies also its effect on the world: "Every eye shall see him, and they also which pierced him, and all kindreds of the earth shall wail because of him."[1] And these sounds continue. Things do not melt quietly into the peace of the kingdom of God. There is a crash of ruin, and a winepress of the wrath of Almighty God, and a lake that burns with fire and brimstone. And this judgment falls, not only on principles and powers of evil, but on nations of men; and not only on nations, but on separate persons, even on "every one who is not found written in the book of life." He who does not accept the reality of the world's rebellion and ruin, and of the wrath and judgment which it brings, must certainly reject this whole book from the canon; and, with it, must tear away large and living portions of every preceding book of Scripture.

6. The features of apocalyptic teaching, which have now been noticed, may serve as instances of the whole character of the doctrine, which is combined with its predictions;

[1] Rev. i. 7.

and which, as a doctrine of consummation, is an evident advance, in that particular direction, on the doctrine of the Epistles. But it is when the prophecy carries us beyond the great crisis, that this advance is most clearly seen. The coming of the Lord is not the last thing which we know. After that event has closed the present age, after the victory has been won, and the judgment has dealt with things that are past, the final results appear, and the true life of man begins. The doctrine of the book is ultimately and pre-eminently one of *restoration.*

"I saw a new heaven and a new earth, for the first heaven and the first earth were passed away, and there was no more sea. And I John saw the holy city, new Jerusalem, coming down from God out of heaven, prepared as a bride adorned for her husband." In taking these words for my text I placed myself at the point where the whole teaching of Scripture culminates. Here, at the last step, we have a definite and satisfactory completion of the former doctrine of the future. There is to be a perfect humanity; not only perfect individually, but perfect in society. There is to be a city of God. "The Holy City!" — there is the realization of the true tendencies of man. "New Jerusalem!" — there is the fulfilment of the ancient promises of God.

Dwell for a moment on the word "city," under the remembrance of what it was to those in whose language the book is written. The city is a constitution of society complete in its own local habitation; the visible collection of buildings being a symbol of the organized life within. It is the most perfect realization, and the most convenient representation, of *society in its maturity;* in which the various relations of men are so combined, as to promote the welfare of the several members, and secure the unity of a common life to the whole. "It is" (as has been said) "the perfecting of the self-provisions of Nature, and the condition of the highest well-being of man."

There is no need to tell how poorly this idea has been realized in fact, nor are the causes of the failure remote from view. In this fallen world all communities have grown up under hard external conditions, and with a deep internal disease, sustaining all sorts of shocks and wounds, and often developing what vigor they possess in forms of violence and oppression. History is the record of human society. There we see

> "The giant forms of empires on their way
> To ruin: one by one
> They tower, and they are gone:"

leaving materials to be combined again, that they may be again dissolved, and forces which renew their eternal struggle at the same time to construct and to destroy. Ever since Cain went forth and builded the first city, the long experiment has continued; and he who surveys the results, in the communities which have filled, and now fill, the habitable world, will return from his inspection wearied and disheartened, and little able to anticipate the perfection of man from the progress of society and the education of the world.

And yet human nature is to find the realization of its tendencies and the fulfilment of its hopes. The Bible opens the prospect of which history had led us to despair. It is one long account of the preparation of the city of God. That is one distinct point of view from which the Bible ought to be regarded, and one from which its contents will appear in clearer light. We are accustomed in the present day to read it too exclusively from the individual point of view, as the record for each man of that will of God and that way of salvation with which he is personally concerned. This it is, but it is more than this. It places before us the restoration, not only of the personal, but of the social life; the creation, not only of the man of God, but of the city of God; and it presents the society or city, not as a mere name for the congregation of individuals, but as having a being and life of its own, in which the Lord finds his satisfaction and man his perfection. The "Jerusalem which is above" is, in relation to the Lord, "the Bride, the Lamb's Wife,"[1] and, in relation to man, it is "the Mother of us all."[2] In its appearance the revealed course of redemption culminates, and the history of man is closed: and thus the last chapters of the Bible declare the unity of the whole book, by completing the design which has been developed in its pages, and disclosing the result to which all preceding steps have tended.[3] Take from the Bible the final vision of the heavenly Jerusalem, and what will have been lost? Not merely a single passage, a

[1] Rev. xxi. 9. [2] Gal. iv. 26.

[3] Πᾶσα πόλις φυσει ἐστιν, εἴπερ καὶ αἱ πρῶται κοινωνίαι· τέλος γὰρ αὕτη ἐκείνων· ἡ δὲ φύσις τέλος ἐστίν· οἷον γὰρ ἕκαστόν ἐστι τῆς γενέσεως τελεσθείσης, ταύτην φαμὲν τὴν φύσιν εἶναι ἑκάστου. . . . καὶ πρότερον δὴ τῇ φύσει πόλις ἢ ἕκαστος ἡμῶν ἔστι, τὸ γὰρ ὅλον πρότερον ἀναγκαῖον εἶναι τοῦ μέρους. "Every state is such by nature, if the primary communities are (such as families); for that is the *end* of *these.* But nature is an *end*, a consummated thing; for what each thing is when its being is completed, that we call its nature. . . . *And surely by its nature a state is prior to every one of us, for the whole is necessarily prior to the part.*" — *Aristot. Polit.* lib i. ch. 1. Most true principles of the true history of man!

sublime description, an important revelation; but a conclusion by which all that went before is interpreted and justified. We shall have an unfinished plan, in which human capacities have not found their full realization, or divine preparations their adequate result. To the mind that looks beyond individual life, or that understands what is necessary to the perfection of individual life, a Bible that did not end by building for us a city of God would appear to leave much in man unprovided for, and much in itself unaccounted for. But as it is, neither of these deficiencies exists. The great consummation is there, and we are instructed to observe, that, from the first, the desires of men and the preparations of God have been alike directed towards it.

At the beginning of the sacred story, the Father of the faithful comes forth into view, followed by those who are heirs with him of the same promise; and they separate themselves to the life of strangers, because they are "looking for a city which hath foundations, whose builder and maker is God." In due time solid pledges of the divine purpose follow. We behold a peculiar people, a divinely-framed polity, a holy city, a house of God. It is a wonderful spectacle — this system of earthly types, thus consecrated and glorified by miraculous interventions and inspired panegyrics. Do we look on the fulfilment of patriarchal hopes, or on the types of their fulfilment? on the final form of human society, or on the figures of the true? The answer was given by Prophets and Psalmists, and then by the word of the Gospel, finally by the hand of God, which swept that whole system from the earth. It was gone when the words of the text were written, and when the closing scene of the Bible presented the new Jerusalem, not as the restoration, but as the antitype of the old.[1]

This vision teaches us, that the drama of the world must be finished, and its dispensation closed, that the Lord must have come, the dead have been raised, the judgment have sat, the heavens and the earth which are now have passed away, and the new creation have appeared, before the chosen people shall see the city of their habitation.

Meantime it is the day of preparation. The builder of the eternal city first "prepares his work without, and makes it fit for himself in the field, and afterwards builds his house."[2] There was much to be done, and it takes long to do it. The members of the intended society must be sorted and collected out of the mass of mankind. They must also be tested and trained. The very grounds on which the future work is to rest must themselves be laid The perfect society is to be founded on men's relations to God, and is to be compacted by their relations to each other. The true relations were destroyed by sin, and it was necessary that they should be constituted afresh.

This is done in Jesus Christ. Propitiation and atone ment, reconciliation and redemption, are words which express the restoration of the broken relations with God, as accomplished by the work of the Mediator. Those who receive Christ Jesus the Lord are thereby in a state of grace. Sin no longer divides and estranges them from God. He has returned to them, and they to him. They have fellowship with the Father and with the Son by the

[1] See Alford's Prolegomena for a brief summary of arguments for the traditional date.

[2] Prov. xxiv. 27.

Holy Ghost. God dwells in them, and they in him. Thus in each separate soul are beforehand established those relations with God in Christ, which shall hereafter glorify the community of the saints, in the day when "the throne of God and of the Lamb shall be in it," and "God himself shall be with them and be their God."

To the reconstitution of men's relations to God must also be added that of their relations to each other. To what an extent these have suffered from the fall of man a glance at the history of the world or at any section of society is sufficient to convince us. Not only the violations, but the very institutions of law and justice testify to the fact; for the law is not made for a righteous man. The inherent vice of human society lies in the depravity of human nature. If that were healed, and transmuted into universal righteousness and love, the internal happiness and perfection would be secured. And they are to be secured in that city, where "the people shall be all righteous,"[1] and where love shall never fail. To the formation of those habits of mind the teaching of God is now visibly directed, and men are trained, on the grounds and motives of the Gospel, to love one another. Love is ever represented as "the end of the commandment," the highest attainment of man, the completion of his education by God. And no wonder it is so represented, since the present prepares the future, and that future is to be a state of society — "a city which is compact together."[2] The Gospel then, which lays in the hearts of those who receive it the deepest grounds of fellowship, and educates them to

[1] Isa. lx. 21. [2] Ps. cxxii. 3.

the habit of love, is visibly preparing the conditions of the things to come. As if to signalize this connection of the present work and the future promise of the Gospel, it is committed to the last Apostle, who closes the Holy Scripture, both to be our chief teacher in the love of the brethren, and to open to our eyes the scene in which it shall be perfected.

Thus does the present world give scope for the preparation of the city of God. Its fundamental principles are being established, its members gathered, trained, and made ready. At the same time all moral tendencies are being wrought out by conflict and experience; and the vanity of what is vain and the evil of what is evil have space to show themselves, before the final fires and the eternal judgment remove them forever from the scene. Then, when Babylon has fallen, the city of God will appear.

Its fabric and scenery are described in symbolic language glowing with all precious and glorious things; nor do we desire an interpreter who will tell us what the symbols severally represent, in the future details of the glorified society. Perhaps such an attempt would impair, rather than enhance, the effect of the vision, which now kindles the imagination of expectant faith by the entire assemblage of its glories. I only dwell upon the fact that it *is a city* which stands before us, as the final home of mankind. If we think only of our individual portion, we miss the completeness of Scripture in its provision for the completeness of man. If individual blessedness were the highest thought of humanity, it might have been sufficient to have restored the lost garden of Eden, and to have left the inhabitants of the new earth to dwell safely in its wildernesses and sleep in its woods.[1] Such dreams of human happiness have haunted the minds of men who have been wearied with the disorders, corruptions, and miseries of society, till society in itself has seemed to them a standing hindrance to perfection, and almost necessarily an organism of evil. Thus the habit of mind which flies from man to nature, and desires unconstrained freedom, and would simplify to the utmost all social relations, has ever looked to depict a heaven of fields and bowers, and to ask for the life of the first Paradise again. It is worthy of remark that the religions of the world have, for the most part, confessed in this way their despair of human society, and unconsciously acknowledged that in their scheme of things the true foundations of it were wanting.

Not so does the revelation of God inform the expectations of those who receive it. Other systems evade the demands of the highest tendencies of man: this provides that they shall be realized. It decrees not only the individual happiness, but the corporate perfection of man; and closes the book of its prophecy by assuring the children of the living God that "*he hath prepared for them a city.*"

The survey which has been made in these Lectures has now carried us from the beginning to the end of the New Testament, from the cradle of Bethlehem to the city of God. We have seen that this collection of various and occasional writings presents to us a gradually progressive scheme, fully wrought out in its several stages, and advancing in a natural order of succession.

First a person is manifested and facts are set forth, in

[1] Ezek. xxxiv. 25.

the simplest external aspect, under the clearest light, and with the concurrence of a fourfold witness. This witness also is itself progressive, and in the last Gospel the glory of the person has grown more bright, and the meaning of the facts more clear.

Then, in the Book of Acts, Christ is preached as perfected, and as the refuge and life of the world. The results of his appearing are summed up and settled; and men are called to believe and be saved. Those who do so find themselves in new relations to each other; they become one body, and grow into the form and life of a Catholic Church.

The state which has thus been entered needs to be expounded, and the life which has been begun needs to be educated. The Apostolic letters perform the work. The questions which universally follow the first submissions of the mind receive their answers, and so the faith which was general grows definite. The rising exigencies of the new life are met, both for the man and for the Church: and we learn what is the happy consciousness, and what the holy conversation, which belong to those who are "*in* Christ Jesus."

Lastly, as members of the body of Christ, we find ourselves partakers in a corporate life and a history larger than our own. We feel that we are taken up into a scheme of things, which is in conflict with the present, and which cannot realize itself here. Therefore our final teaching is by prophecy, which shows us, not how we are personally saved and victorious, but how the battle goes upon the whole; and which issues in the appearance of a holy city, in which redemption reaches its end, and the Redeemer finds his joy; in which human tendencies are realized, and divine promises fulfilled; in which the ideal has become the actual, and man is perfected in the presence and glory of God.

If this doctrine is not of the world, every step that it takes in advance must make that fact more plain. The world feels that it is so. The manifestation of Christ it will admire and interpret for itself. The preaching of Christ it can hear and accept in its generality. The life in Christ through the Spirit it cannot receive. The kingdom of Christ in its antagonism to itself it cannot suffer. Yes, the world is right. In following the advancing line of doctrine in the Scriptures, we diverge further and further from its paths and habits of thought. But is that a subject of regret? What has been the progress of doctrine achieved by the spirit which is of the world? Into what can it ever lead our souls? Into vague desires to which nothing corresponds, into great ideas which remain ideas still, into uncertainty and perplexity, into vanity and vexation of spirit. Only the written word of God, confidingly followed in the progressive steps of its advance, can lead the weakest or the wisest into the deep blessedness of the life that is in Christ, and into the final glory of the city of God.

Perhaps in some minds this needful confidence may be strengthened by a review of the books of the New Testament in the light in which they have now been placed. When it is felt that these narratives, letters, and visions do in fact fulfil the several functions, and sustain the mutual relations, which would belong to the parts of one design, coalescing into a doctrinal scheme, which is orderly, progressive, and complete, then is the mind of the reader in conscious contact with the mind of God; then the superficial diversity of the parts is lost in the essential unity of the whole: the many writings have become one Book; the many writers have become one Author. From the position of students, who address themselves with critical interest to the works of Matthew, of Paul, or of John, we have risen to the higher level of believers, who open with holy joy "the New Testament of our Lord and Saviour Jesus Christ," and, while we receive from his own hand the book of life eternal, we hear him saying still, "**I have given unto them the words which thou gavest me.**"

NOTES.

NOTES.

PREFACE.

NOTE I., p. 13.

FOR the customary order of the books of the New Testament in ancient times we may refer to Manuscripts, Catalogues, and Old Versions.

The testimony of Manuscripts will be at once exhibited and certified by the following extract from Mr. Scrivener's *Introduction to the Criticism of the New Testament.*

"It is right to bear in mind that comparatively few copies of the whole [Greek] New Testament remain; the usual practice being to write the four Gospels in one volume, the Acts and Epistles in another: manuscripts of the Apocalypse, which was little used for public worship, being much rarer than those of the other books. Occasionally the Gospels, Acts, and Epistles form a single volume; sometimes the Apocalypse is added to other books. . . . The Codex Sinaiticus of Tischendorf is the more precious, that it happily exhibits the whole New Testament complete: so would the Codices Alexandrinus and Ephraemi, but they are sadly mutilated. No other uncial copies have this advantage, and very few cursives. In England, only four such are known. . . . Besides these Scholtz enumerates only nineteen foreign copies of the whole New Testament; but twenty-seven in all out of the whole mass of extant documents.

"Whether copies contain the whole or a part of the sacred volume, *the general order of the books is the following: Gospels, Acts, Catholic Epistles, Pauline Epistles, Apocalypse.* A solitary manuscript of the fifteenth century (Venet. 10, Evan. 209) places the Gospels between the Pauline Epistles and the Apocalypse: in the

Codices Sinaiticus, Leicestrensis, Fabri (Evan. 90), and Montfortianus, as in the Bodleian Canonici 34, the Pauline Epistles *precede* the Acts; the Codex Basiliensis (No. 4 of the Epistles), and Lambeth 1182, 1183, have the Pauline Epistles immediately after the Acts and before the Catholic Epistles, as in our present Bibles; Scholz's Evan. 368 stands thus, St. John's Gospel, Apocalypse, then all the Epistles; in Havniens. I. No. 234 of the Gospels (A. D. 1278), the order appears to be, Acts, Pauline Epistles, Catholic Epistles, Gospels; in Basil. B. vi. 27 or Cod. 1, the Gospels now follow the Acts and the Epistles; while in Evan. 51 the *binder* has set the Gospels last; these however are mere accidental exceptions to the prevailing rule. *The four Gospels are almost invariably found in their familiar order*, although in the Codex Bezæ they stand, Matthew, John, Luke, Mark; in the Codex Monacensis (X), John, Luke, Matthew, Mark; in the Curetonian Syriac version, Matthew, Mark, John, Luke. In the Pauline Epistles, that to the Hebrews precedes the four Pastoral Epistles, and immediately follows the second to the Thessalonians in the four great Codices, Sinaiticus, Alexandrinus, Vaticanus, and Ephraem: in the copy from which the Cod. Vatican. was taken, the Hebrews followed the Galatians. The Codex Claromontanus, the document next in importance to these four, sets the Colossians appropriately enough next to its kindred and contemporaneous Epistle to the Ephesians, but postpones that to the Hebrews to Philemon, as in our present Bibles; an arrangement which at first, no doubt, originated in the early scruples prevailing in the *Western* Church with respect to the authorship and canonical authority of that divine Epistle."[1]

From extant *Manuscripts* I turn to the earliest *Catalogues* of the sacred books which occur in the writings of Christian antiquity, and these, perhaps, are more real indications of habit in the Church than particular manuscripts can be. It will only be necessary to advert to a few of the most important of these Catalogues, and in so doing I refer the reader to the Rev. B. F. Westcott's *History of the Canon of the New Testament*, or his shorter and more popular volume, *The Bible in the Church*, books which deal with a subject

1 *Introduction to the Criticism of the New Testament*, pp. 60-62.

lying close to the foundations of our faith, in a spirit not less reverential than critical, and which place within the reach of ordinary readers an exact, lucid, and succinct account of a history which was before the property of the learned.

The Muratorian Fragment, "of which the date may be fixed with tolerable certainty, A. D. 160–170," and which "may be regarded on the whole as a summary of the opinion of the Western Church on the canon shortly after the middle of the second century, commences with the last words of a sentence which evidently referred to the Gospel of St. Mark:" the Gospel of St. Luke is then expressly mentioned as "the third," and the Gospel of St. John "as the fourth." The Book of Acts is mentioned next, and then thirteen Epistles of St. Paul, enumerated in the following order: Corinthians I., II., Ephesians, Philippians, Colossians, Galatians, Thessalonians I., II., Romans, Epistles (it is observed) written (like those in the Apocalypse) to seven churches; then Philemon, Titus, Timothy I., II. After observations on these books, the Fragment diverges to spurious or disputed books, and the assertion that the Epistle of Jude and two Epistles of John are reckoned among the Catholic (Epistles) is the only notice of the remaining books which its corrupt and apparently mutilated state has left.

The Catalogue given by Eusbeius (H. E. iii. 25), *c.* A. D. 340, claims a special importance on account of his having been employed by Constantine to prepare the first edition of the Bible which had the seal of a central or sovereign authority. The order is the same as our own, except in as far as it appears disarranged by the principle on which the Catalogue is formed, namely, that of distinguishing the acknowledged from the controverted books.

"First, then, we place the holy quaternion of the Gospels, which are followed by the account of the Acts of the Apostles. After this we must reckon the Epistles of St. Paul; and next to them we must maintain as genuine the Epistle circulated as the former of John, and in like manner that of Peter. In addition to these books, if possibly such a view seem correct, we must place the Revelation of John, the judgments on which we shall set forth in due course, and these are regarded as generally received. Among the controverted books, which are nevertheless well known and recognized by most, we class the Epistle circulated under the name of James, and that of Jude, as well as the Second of Peter, and the so-called Second and Third of John, whether they really belong to that Evangelist or possibly to another of the same name."[1]

The Catalogue of Athanasius (Ep. Alex. 326) A. D. 373, given in a style of authoritative decision, is as follows: "The Books of the New Testament are these, —Four Gospels, according to Matthew, Mark, Luke, John. Then after these, the Acts of the Apostles, and the so-called Catholic Epistles of Apostles, seven in number; thus, of James, one; of Peter, two; of John, three; and after these, of Jude, one. In addition to these there are fourteen Epistles of the Apostle Paul, in their order written thus: Romans, Corinthians I., II., Galatians, Ephesians, Philippians, Colossians, Thessalonians I., II., and that to the Hebrews; and in succession, Timothy I., II., Titus, Philemon; and again the Apocalypse of John."[2]

The testimonies of Eusebius and Athanasius are in effect those of the Greek and Alexandrine Churches. One other list promulgated a few years later (A. D. 397) by the voice of a whole province, is on that account worthy to be specified, since it is the first (certain) synodical decision on the canon of Scripture. It is found in the proceedings of the third Council of Carthage, at which Augustine was present. The order is as follows: "Four books of the Gospels, one book of the Acts of the Apostles, thirteen Epistles of the Apostle Paul, one Epistle of the same to the Hebrews, two Epistles of the Apostle Peter, three of John, one of James, one of Jude, one book of the Apocalypse of John;"[3] precisely corresponding to our own order, except in the place given to the Epistle of James. Lastly, as the best witness of Italian custom we may take the Catalogue of Ruffinus (*c.* A. D. 410), in which the order is identical with that of the decree of Carthage, and therefore with our own, save that the Catholic Epistles stand as follows: "Two of the Apostle Peter; one of James, the Lord's brother and Apostle; one of Jude; three of John."

But perhaps the most important evidence to the custom of the

1 *History of Canon*, 481-2. 2 *Ibid.* 574. 3 *Ibid.* 509.

Church is not that of manuscripts or catalogues, but rather that of the two venerable versions of Syria and North Africa, which are almost coeval with the first general recognition of a collected New Testament. The Peshito was popularly and practically the Bible of the Syrian Church. The Old Latin was, as it were, the parent of the Vulgate, which became the common Bible of the West. The order of the Peshito is the same as that of the best Greek manuscripts, the four Gospels, the Acts, the Catholic Epistles (i. e. those which it admitted), the Epistles of St. Paul (the Apocalypse being absent). The order of the Vulgate is that which our modern Bibles exhibit; the Old Latin order of the Gospels, Matthew, John, Mark, and Luke (which was ruled no doubt by the apostolic rank of the authors), being changed by Jerome in accordance with the Greek order, which was derived not merely from chronological considerations, but from a finer doctrinal instinct.

This glance at the various testimonies which survive, of the ancient customs of the Church, is sufficient to show that the order with which we are familiar has substantially prevailed from the first recognition of the separate books as forming one collection or instrument. The great divisions, the Gospels, the Acts, the Epistles, and the Apocalypse, occur habitually in their natural order, and though there are many variations (most frequently in regard to the position of the Acts, yet they are exceptions to the general rule. The books which compose these several divisions likewise assume habitually the same arrangement as at present. It is so with the four Gospels, and with the Pauline Epistles, the order of which is seldom varied except in respect of the place given to the Hebrews. The only important variation, which obtains extensively, is in the relative positions of the Pauline and Catholic Epistles. The Manuscripts for the most part place the Catholic Epistles next to the Acts, and before the Pauline Epistles. In the Catalogues the opposite order is more frequent, and becomes increasingly so the farther we advance. Of five-and-twenty Catalogues which are collected in the Appendix to Mr. Westcott's *History of the Canon*, ranging from c. A. D. 170 to A. D. 636, I find that seven give the first place to the Catholic, and eighteen to the Pauline Epistles.

This last point is one of minor importance, yet as connected with the conformation of the New Testament it has its interest; and as some little stress is laid upon it in one of these Lectures (the VIth), it may be well to point out the following reasons for the greater fitness of the arrangement which has upon the whole prevailed.

1. There is the closest possible relation between the Book of Acts and St. Paul's Epistles, the latter part of the Book forming as it were the historical introduction to his writings, so that we pass from one to the other by a natural — it almost might seem a necessary — transition.

2. The unity and mass of St. Paul's writings properly claim for them precedence over the fewer, shorter, and less connected writings.

3. The course of doctrinal instruction pleads for the same arrangement, in order that the more thorough and systematic treatment of fundamental subjects may precede that which is more supplementary.

4. In the heart of the Catholic Epistles, there is a note which seems to appoint their position, namely, in the reference (2 Pet. iii. 15, 16) to St. Paul's writings as previously known, and in the express intimation of an intention to confirm their doctrine.

These considerations obviously outweigh the one reason for the opposite order, which is found in the relative historical positions of the authors, and which, taken by itself, would certainly postpone the productions of the later Apostle, born out of due time, to those which bear the names of chief members of the original college.

LECTURE I.

NOTE II., p. 39.

IN his recently published *Apologia*, Dr. Newman has shown into what form he has found it necessary to recast his doctrine of Development, though the subject is touched in a shy and uneasy manner.

"It (i. e. the Infallible Power which imposes doctrine) must ever profess to be guided by Scripture and tradition. It must refer to the particular Apostolic truth which it is enforcing or (what is called) *defining*. Nothing, then, can be presented to me in time to come as part of the faith, but what I ought already to have received, and have not actually received, (if not) merely because it had not been told me. . . . It must be what I may even have guessed or wished to be included in the Apostolic revelation. . . Perhaps I and others actually have always believed it, and the only question which is now decided in my behalf is that I am henceforth to believe that I am only holding what the Apostles held before me."[1]

These statements are then expressly applied to "the doctrine which Protestants consider our greatest difficulty, that of the Immaculate Conception;" and, after assuring us that the imposition of this doctrine is no burden to himself or others, and that he "sincerely thinks that St. Bernard and St. Thomas, who scrupled at it in their day, had they lived into this would have rejoiced to accept it for its own sake," he adds the remark that "the number of those (so-called) new doctrines will not oppress us, if it takes eight centuries to promulgate even one of them. Such is about the length of time through which the preparation has been carried on for the definition of the Immaculate Conception."[2]

These expressions occur incidentally while the author is showin that "the (so-called) new doctrines" are "no burden" to priests under the Roman obedience, which of course is true, if the doc-

[1] Part vii. p. 393.

[2] p. 395.

trines be such as they "have *guessed and wished* to be included in the Apostolic revelation." But the expressions themselves are remarkable as showing how awkwardly Dr. Newman's own doctrine of Development has assumed the garb and style of his Church's doctrine of tradition; *his* true account of a development which historically took place, veiling itself, as by command, under *its* fiction of a tradition which did not really exist.

A doctrine is for the first time promulgated by the Infallible Authority, and imposed as an article of the faith. "The preparation for it has been carried on for eight hundred years." Eight hundred years ago is the most distant point at which any "*preparation*" for it can be discerned, that "preparation" being found in the first suggestion of the opinion, and in the rejection of it by the leading authorities of the time as new and false; but as time goes on it gains influence and acceptance. It is ackdowledged, then, that *in the thousand years preceding it was not even in preparation*, that there is no trace of it whatever until its mediæval dawn. According to the doctrine of Development, the Infallible Authority would decree its truth as having been gradually wrought out during those eight hundred years, and at last adequately recognized by the instinct of the Church. According to the doctrine of Tradition, it must decree the truth of the opinion on the ground of its having been a part of the original revelation handed down from the beginning. In the one case it would affirm that the doctrine *would have been* held by the Apostles if they had known of it. In the other case it must affirm that the doctrine *was* made known to the Apostles and that they *did* hold it. To this latter theory Dr. Newman has now seen it necessary to conform his language. "The *only* question *now decided* is that he is holding *what the Apostles held* before him." The Infallible Authority is thus recognized, not as deciding on the truth of an opinion, but as certifying a *fact*, i. e. that the Apostles held such and such an opinion as part of the revelation given to them. If no evidence of this fact survives, if no tradition has handed it down, if the doctrine is one which only *began* to be *prepared* eight hundred years ago, it is evident that the Infallible Authority can only have known the fact which it certifies by a direct revelation.

T: one who considers the exigencies of the Romish position so glaringly exemplified in connection with the doctrine here alluded to, it must appear that this issue of an attempt to provide for those exigencies, by a theory in some measure accordant with facts, is the strongest testimony to the ineradicable sense of Christendom, that the divine communication of truth was limited to the Apostolic age.

The method of the perpetuation and transmission of the truths then communicated is of course an entirely separate question. But whether that question be determined as it is by Rome, or as it is by us, the kind of development of doctrine which legitimately belongs to the Church must be, on either hypothesis, theoretically the same. It must consist in a fuller and more systematic apprehension of the truths which were communicated at first, not in the addition of truths communicated afterwards. Practically, the Church of Rome has acted (as Dr. Newman so distinctly felt) on the latter, and *not* on the former, of these principles: first adding new doctrines on the most flimsy pretences of a tradition, and then superadding one for which not the slenderest thread of a tradition could be shown.

LECTURE II.

NOTE III., p. 60.

No more interesting and suggestive summary of the comparative character and scope of the several Gospels could be given, than that which is produced by simply placing their respective conclusions side by side.

MATT. xxviii. 18–20.

Jesus came and spake unto them, saying, All power is given unto me in heaven and in earth.

Go ye therefore, and teach all nations, baptizing them in the name of the Father, and of the Son, and of the Holy Ghost:

Teaching them to observe all things whatsoever I have commanded you: and, lo, I am with you alway, even unto the end of the world. Amen.

MARK xvi. 15–20.

And he said unto them, Go ye into all the world, and preach the gospel to every creature.

He that believeth and is baptized shall be saved; but he that believeth not shall be damned.

And these signs shall follow them that believe; In my name shall they cast out devils; they shall speak with new tongues,

They shall take up serpents; and if they drink any deadly thing, it shall not hurt them; they shall lay hands on the sick, and they shall recover.

So then after the Lord had spoken unto them, he was received up into heaven, and sat on the right hand of God.

And they went forth, and preached everywhere, the Lord working with them, and confirming the word with signs following. Amen.

LUKE xxiv. 50–53.

And he led them out as far as to Bethany, and he lifted up his hands, and blessed them.

And it came to pass, while he blessed them, he was parted from them, and carried up into heaven.

And they worshipped him, and returned to Jerusalem with great joy:

And were continually in the temple, praising and blessing God. Amen.

JOHN xx. 28–31.

And Thomas answered and said unto him, My Lord and my God.

Jesus saith unto him, Thomas, because thou hast seen me, thou hast believed: blessed are they that have not seen, and yet have believed.

And many other signs truly did Jesus in the presence of his disciples, which are not written in this book:

But these are written, that ye might believe that Jesus is the Christ, the Son of God; and that believing ye might have life through his name.

Here we see, 1. In St. Matthew, the Royal Lawgiver, or King and Teacher of men, endued with all authority,[1] founding a kingdom for all nations, with its ordinance of admission (baptism) and its permanent laws ("Whatsoever I have commanded you"): and still the *kingdom* is (as it were) a *school*, in which his commissioners are charged to continue the work of teaching which he had begun.[2]

2. In St. Mark the Mighty Worker, who leaves the energy of his action in his Church. Not here is represented the slower process of forming and training communities, but the bold and world-wide proclamation, with the sure execution of its sanction.[3] Then the signs of living power are to follow those that believe, beginning with the casting out of devils in his name. Finally, the scene is changed in a moment, and the command and promise are seen in their fulfilment—the Lord in heaven, the disciples on earth—they going forth and preaching everywhere, and the Lord still working with them and confirming the word by the signs of power.

3. In St. Luke, the Friend of Man, sending to all nations the message of repentance and remission of sins, and ensuring to his messengers the promise of his Father; while the reality of kind companionship is preserved to the end, in the mention of localities, movements, and gestures ("He led them out as far as to Bethany," "He lifted up His hands and blessed them," "He was parted from them"), the parting itself being one of love (while He blessed them), and one which leaves behind it a state of worship and joy.

4. In St. John, the Son of God, receiving from the lately doubting disciple the highest acknowledgment which had yet come from human lips, "My Lord and my God,"[4] and then, as it were, lifting up his eyes beyond the little company who had seen him, and pronouncing for all ages and nations a blessing on those who, not having seen, should yet have believed. Yet farther, the Evangelist speaks from himself, thus characteristically closing the only gospel in which the thoughts of the writer have been mingled with his

1 *ἐξουσία.* 2 *μαθητεύσατε—διδάσκοντες.*

3 Compare the *μαθητεύσατε πάντα τὰ ἔθνη* with the *κηρύξατε πάσῃ τῇ κτίσει.*

4 ὁ Κύριός μου καὶ ὁ Θεός μου.

narrative. He tells us that he has given us incidents intentionally selected for a certain definite purpose, namely, to present the great object of faith in his highest character as the Son of God, and so to secure the result of faith in its deepest essence, "life through his name."

NOTE IV., p. 66.

This effect of the opening of St. Matthew's Gospel, and so of the whole Gospel record, is well described by Lange:

"The genealogy, &c., with which the Gospel according to Matthew opens, is of the greatest importance. The first Gospel connects the New Testament with the Old, not by giving an index of the writings of the Old Testament, but by delineating the Old Testament genealogy of Jesus. This serves not merely as evidence of the indissoluble connection between the Old and the New Testament, which continued in the secret recesses of Jewish life even during the age of the Apocrypha, but expresses the important truth that God revealed himself and carried on his covenant purposes, not only by the spoken and written word, but also and chiefly in and by the seed of Abraham, until he came in whom both impersonation and revelation had reached their climax.

"In the Gospel by Matthew the life of Jesus is presented as forming part of the history and life of the Jewish nation; and hence as the historical fulfilment of the blessing promised to Abraham and to his seed. Jesus is here set before us as the new-born King of the Jews, as the promised Messiah, and the aim and goal of every progressive stage of the theocracy. He is the great Antitype of Old Testament history, in whom everything has been fulfilled — the types in the law, in worship, in historical events, and in gracious interpositions — in short, the fulfilment of the theocracy. In and with him the old covenant passes into the new, the theocracy into the kingdom of heaven, the demands of the law into the beatitudes, Sinai into the Mount of Beatitudes, the prophetic into the teaching office, the priesthood into redemption by suffering, and the kingship into the triumph of almighty grace, restoring, helping, and delivering a fallen world."[1]

[1] Lange, *Commentary on St. Matthew*, pp. 49, 50.

Again, in his other work, the same thoughts occur:—

"He (St. Matthew) exhibits the Gospel in its historical relation as the completion, the spiritual fruit of the Christological growth in the Old Testament. It was his task to prove to his own nation that Jesus was the Messiah, the Son of David, the Son of Abraham. (Chap. i. 1.) But just because Christ was, in his eyes, the true and spiritual King of the Jews, and His kingdom the true theocratic kingdom of God, did Matthew from the very first give prominence to the great contrast between the spiritual Israel and the worldly and hardened Israel. Thence it was that from the beginning new conflicts were ever arising, thence that we continually meet with fresh sufferings of the holy Heir of the ancient theocracy till His death upon the cross, new triumphs till the manifestation of His glory. The series of the Messiah's sufferings runs through the whole of this gospel as its prevailing thought."[1]

NOTE V., p. 71.

The essential identity of the synoptist view of the person of Christ with that given by St. John is ably asserted by Dorner. It may be well to cite a part of his argument:—

"Taking the notices of the Synoptists together, it thus appears that for all eternity, also for the eternal life[2] in heaven, the Person of Christ, the Son of God and the Son of Man, forms the centre point of the Christian religion, in the trials and in the triumphs of individuals and of the Church. He is the perfect Lawgiver. He not merely reveals, but he realizes as well, the holy and just as the gracious will of God; hence is He also the Judge of the world. He has and exercises power over the whole world, even as he does over the spiritual; He communicates here the forgiveness of sins and the Holy Ghost, there eternal felicity; and the summit of the latter is ever formed by perfect fellowship with His Person. . . .

"It may be boldly affirmed that the entire representation of Christ given by the Synoptists may be placed by the side of the Johannine as perfectly identical inasmuch as faith, moulded by

1 Life of Christ, vol. i. 249.

2 ζωὴ αἰώνιος.

means of the synoptic tradition, must have essentially the same features in its conception of Christ as the Christ of John has.

"The passages in John which speak the most loftily of Christ are those to which the Synoptists supply exactly the closest parallels, whilst some of the strongest traits in the latter find no parallel in John; comp. Matt. ix. 2-6 with John v. 41 (viii. 11), Matt. xxviii. 18-20 with John iii. 35. But as these latter synoptic traits are assuredly capable of being without difficulty incorporated with John's representation of Christ, so, on the other hand, may what John, with Paul and the Epistle to the Hebrews, advances, that goes beyond the synoptists — that, namely, which has relation to the element of pre-existence — be brought into relation to them. The Christ of the Synoptists stands already so high above the Ebionitic Christ; He is especially through His eschatological aspect so linked with the world-idea, that to the synoptic faith there needs to be added not so much a new object as simply a stronger interest of gnosis; and so also it is that this faith can find satisfaction in no narrower utterance concerning Christ than in such a one as the dogma of His pre-existence will enunciate.

"In point of fact there are not wanting in the Synoptists themselves the beginning of such: comp. Luke vii. 37, Matt. xi. 19, where Christ calls himself the Wisdom, with Prov. viii., Matt. xi. 27; especially, however, Luke xi. 49 with Matt. xxiii. 34, Matt. xiii. 17, Luke x. 23-24, with John viii. 56 ff."[1]

LECTURE III.

NOTE VI., p. 95.

This hindrance is strongly put in some words of Dräseke quoted by Stier: —

"The old Messiah in the flesh is with them; *therefore* the new Comforter, the Spirit, is far from them. What hindered their being comforted? Jesus himself, who, comforting, stood before

1 Dorner, On the Person of Christ, Introduction, pp. 60, 61.

them, was the hindrance! As long as he, this Messiah, bearing all the prophetic marks upon him, stood before them in person, this his person continued to be a foundation and prop to that system of vanities which bewitched their heads and hearts. The Form must pass away from their eyes before the Spirit could enter their souls. It was good for them that Jesus should go away. Before he, the Christ after the flesh, went away, the Christ after the Spirit could not come. When the former vanished, the latter appeared."[1]

LECTURE IV.

NOTE VII., p. 103.

Baumgarten's *Apostolic History* starts at once from the right point of view; and the effect of this is felt through the whole work. I subjoin a part of his criticism on the cardinal expression, which indicates the relation between the two histories treated by St. Luke, in support of that view of it which is briefly given in the text of the lecture: —

"From the words, 'which Jesus began both to do and to teach,'[1] we perceive that, through the Gospel, St. Luke intends Jesus to be regarded as the acting subject of this history. Consequently, whatever else the Gospel narrates, whether the actions of other persons or the sufferings of the Saviour himself, his labors, either in doing or in teaching, are to be considered as the central point from which the whole is determined. But now it is of especial significance that in this passage there occurs a word which, corresponding to the term πρῶτον, refers us with equal precision, as well to what follows, as to what precedes. It is the word ἤρξατο. With good reason has Meyer maintained that this word has a peculiar emphasis, and has therefore rightly rejected all such expositions of it as would explain away its force. But the explanation which he himself proposes is equally fatal to the emphatic character

1 *Words of the Lord Jesus*, vol. vi. p. 337.

2 ὧν ἤρξατο ὁ Ἰησοῦς ποιεῖν τε καὶ διδάσκειν

which he claims for it. He sees in it, for instance, an antithesis of this kind, 'Jesus began — the Apostles carried on.' But the peculiar force, which Meyer has just claimed for ἤρξατο (began), depends, so far as I can see, on its *position*, standing as it does before the name, which, in itself, comprises the whole subject-matter of the Gospel. . . .

"The impressive force of the word ἤρξατο will, therefore, be duly appreciated as soon as, with Olshausen (in loc.) and Schneckenburger, we regard it as characterizing and referring to the whole of Jesus' labors during his existence on earth — in other words, as describing the whole course of his labors up to the time of his ascension as *initiatory and preparatory.*

"If, therefore, at the commencement of a second book, all that had been narrated in the first is characterized as the work of the initiatory labors of Jesus, is not this a plain intimation that in the second book we are to look for an account of the further continuance of those labors?"[1]

NOTE VIII., p. 112.

The view, which is given in the text, of St. Paul's testimony, concerning the sources from which he had derived his gospel, and particularly of his assertion, 1 Cor. xi. 23, was not reached without some hesitation. It had once seemed to me (as probably it does to most readers) that the interpretation of the words ἐγὼ παρέλαβον ἀπὸ τοῦ Κυρίου, was decided by the more definite language of Gal. i. 12; and also that the express mention both of the ἐγὼ and the κύριος was more natural, on the supposition that the Apostle meant to intimate an immediate personal communication from the Lord to himself. The first of these reasons is removed, if the expressions in the Corinthians on the one hand, and those in the Galatians and Ephesians on the other, contemplate the Gospel (as they obviously do) from the two different sides of history and doctrine. The second reason was merely a confirmation of an interpretation accepted upon other grounds, and has no great force

[1] Baumgarten's *Apostolic History* (Clarke's Tr.), sect. 1, pp. 10, 11.

by itself. It is an argument of the same kind, but perhaps of scarcely as much weight, as that which is adduced on the other side from the use of ἀπό instead of παρά. Dean Alford's decision (the opposite of that which is adopted in the lecture) seems to me too hastily given in regard to a point of so much interest; and he treats the question of the preposition too slightingly:—

"FOR I (no emphasis on ἐγὼ as Meyer, al., see ch. vii. 28 compared with 32; Gal. vi. 17; Phil. iv. 11) RECEIVED FROM THE LORD (*by special revelation*, see Gal. i. 12). Meyer attempts to deny that this revelation was made to Paul himself, on the strength of ἀπό meaning *indirect*, παρά *direct* reception from any one: but this distinction is fallacious: *e. g.* 1 John i. 5, αὕτη ἐστὶν ἡ ἐπαγγελία ἣν ἀκηκόαμεν ἀπ' αὐτοῦ. He supposes that it was made to Ananias or some other, and communicated to Paul. But the sole reason for this somewhat culmsy hypothesis is the supposed force of the preposition, which has no existence. If the Apostle had referred only to the Evangelical tradition or writings (?) he would not have used the first person *singular*, but παρελάβομεν."[1]

"The supposed force of the preposition, which has no existence," is an over-confident expression. Against this decision must be weighed the opinion given by others, *e. g.* by Winer: "After verbs of receiving, &c., ἀπό has merely the general meaning of *whence:* Matt. xvii. 25, ἀπὸ τίνων λαμβάνουσι τέλη; it is *kings* who are the λαμβάνοντες; παρά would have indicated the *immediate* gathering of the taxes, and would have been employed in this passage had the tax-gatherers been spoken of as the λαμβάνοντες. In the expression λαμβάνοντες παρά τινος the τις denotes the person actually delivering or tendering: in λαμβάνοντες ἀπό τινος it denotes merely the proprietor. . . . Paul, in 1 Cor. xi. 23, writes παρέλαβον ἀπὸ τοῦ Κυρίου, 'I received of the Lord,' *not*, the Lord himself has directly, personally, in an ἀποκάλυψις, communicated it to me."[2]

Winer's judgment is adopted by Bishop Ellicott. On Gal. 12, οὐδὲ γὰρ ἐγὼ παρὰ ἀνθρώπου παρέλαβον, he says, "παρὰ ἀνθρώπου 'from man,' not synonymous with ἀπὸ ἀνθρώπου, the distinction between the prepositions after verbs of receiving, &c. (παρὰ more *immediate*, ἀπὸ more

1 Alford in loc. 2 *Grammar of N. T. Diction*, p. 388.

remote source), being apparently regularly maintained in St. Paul's Epistles. Compare 1 Cor. xi. 23, παρέλαβον ἀπὸ τοῦ Κυρίου, on which Winer (*De Verb. Comp. Fasc.* ii., p. 7) rightly observes, 'non παρὰ τοῦ Κυρίου, propterea quod non ipse Christus præsentem docuit.'"

The example given by Alford on the other side appears of little value, as the ἐπαγγελία ἣν ἀκηκόαμεν ἀπ' αὐτοῦ is not a saying cited by St. John as uttered to him personally by the mouth of Christ, but a general summary of the message with which the teachers of the Church were entrusted by their Lord. On the whole, the force of the preposition may be stated thus: it does not *compel* us to adopt either interpretation, but it is more accurate, more natural, and more in accordance with the usage of Scripture, when interpreted not in the sense of an immediate, but of a more remote reception. If we should probably conclude that the general *facts* of the Gospel history (*e.g.* those mentioned in 1 Cor. xv. 3–7) were not communicated to St. Paul by direct revelation, we should have no reason to suppose an exception in regard to the *facts* of the institution of the Lord's Supper; unless the language employed in regard to that subject obliged us to do so. Apparently that is not the case, the preposition used agreeing rather with the opposite opinion, and certainly not being that which would seem likely to have been chosen, if it had been the purpose of the writer to assert the exceptional nature of this particular communication. Thus the addition of ἀπὸ τοῦ Κυρίου to παρέλαβον will only indicate the importance of the acts and words of the institution, as handed down by the known will, and (probably) by the express charge, of the Lord.

In regard to the whole question of the sources of St. Paul's doctrine, it seems to me that his own expressions lead us to class them as follows: (1) the report of others, conveying to him the historical facts of the manifestation of Christ; (2) direct and definite revelations from the Lord Jesus, ascertaining to him the main features of the doctrine which it was his special work to deliver; (3) a general inspiration or guidance of the Holy Ghost, present in his experience, in the workings of his own mind, and more particularly in his study of the Old Testament Scriptures.

The last mentioned method of illumination is evidently of a progressive character. In reference to this subject Ellicott's observation, in his comment on Gal. i. 12, is fair and reasonable: —

"It is a subject of continual discussion, whether the teaching of St. Paul was the result of one single illumination, or of progressive development. The most natural opinion would certainly seem to be this: that as, on the one hand, we may reverently presume that all the fundamental truths of the Gospel would be *fully* revealed to St. Paul, before he commenced preaching; so, on the other, it might have been ordained, that, in accordance with the laws of our spiritual nature, its deepest mysteries and profoundest harmonies should be seen and felt through the practical experiences of his apostolical labors."

I would only wish to add to this statement of the case a distinct mention of that continuous ministration of the Old Testament Scriptures to his mind, which is perceptible in all his writings, and to which attention is called in Note XII.

NOTE IX., p. 120.

Every day we become more familiar with that view of the Apostolic writings, which distinguishes between the narrator and the commentator, assigning a commanding authority to the bare witness of facts, of sayings of the Lord, and of revelations distinctly asserted, and denying such authority to the expositions of the doctrine involved in those facts, sayings, and revelations. In the one department of their work they are true witnesses, delivering to us the words of God. In the other they are fallible men, theorizing or theologizing under the mingled advantages and disadvantages which might result from their historical position. This bisection (if I may use the word) of the testimony of our appointed teachers, leaves us the divine foundations of a theology, but sweeps away the divine theology itself, which they were laid to support. We are at full liberty to raise other edifices in its stead, or, which will be better still, we may leave the materials unused and the ground unoccupied. The intimations of this view of the inspired writings are often hurtful, only because they are disguised; the theory not being avowed, while the language appropriate to it is used. It will be well to keep the theory itself distinctly in sight.

as it will explain the meaning and expose the tendency of many arguments and insinuations which might else make injurious impressions on unestablished faith. Perhaps this theory cannot be better exhibited than in the following words of one of its leading advocates: —

"As to what especially concerns the religious doctrines contained in the Bible, it is clear, from the very nature of the case, that we are only bound to notice those doctrines which can be directly referred to inspiration. We therefore need pay no regard to those doctrines which lay no claim to be considered as inspired, and do not come before us as forming part of a Divine revelation. Such, for instance, are the doctrines of the Mosaic cosmogony, the simple historical narratives in both the Testaments, &c. Above all, those parts of the Bible which *cannot* be directly derived from inspiration, consequently everything in the writings of the *prophets* (and, taking the word in a wide sense, of the *apostles* also) which is in any degree of a a scientific character, the result of reflection, and in any sense whatever the work of science, true and important as it may be, these, one and all, have not a binding authority upon us. But further, *all developments of doctrine*, which were in point of fact the commencement of a theology, have a large margin belonging to them. Take, for instance, the *theological theories* and *peculiar views* of Paul and John, although in *another* regard they have an especial value for us, yet *per se* they are *not revelation.* Their authors worked them out with much *painful* thought, and their thought we also truly regard, when striving like them to master the subject; yet they never claim for their theological deductions a binding authority upon others. On the other hand, all the *direct* declarations in Holy Scripture about our salvation, all the great historical facts of the great drama of revelation, especially the contents of the Gospels, these have all a binding authority upon us. These are the points on which Paul and John theologize.

"It is this assertion of the *comparative* authority of the Holy Scriptures which is the only means of securing them from forced and violent interpretations."[1] It would be more true to say — of exposing them to such interpretations.

[1] R. Rothe, in an article in *Studien und Kritiken*, 1860.

NOTE X., p. 126.

"*If such a spirit did not dwell in the Church, the Bible would not be inspired; for the Bible is, before all things, the written voice of the congregation.* Bold as such a theory of inspiration may sound, it was the earliest creed of the Church, and it is the only one to which the facts of Scripture answer. The Sacred Writers acknowledge themselves men of like passions with ourselves, and we are promised illumination from the Spirit which dwelt in them."[1]

These words of Dr. Williams give a distinct statement of a view of the Holy Scriptures, which is often presented in more ambiguous language. The Bible is the voice of the congregation, in the sense of being a voice *adopted* by the congregation, as the expression of its mind forever; and assertions may be made concerning the Scriptures, which are true in this sense, while they are false in the sense which they are meant to bear: but this sense is here disclaimed by the words "before all things," which deny that the Scriptures have *any character antecedent to this.* This denial flatly contradicts the real voice of the congregation, which has always acknowledged and adopted the Scriptures, in the character of a voice which came to it, not in that of a voice which proceeded from it. Nothing is more certain than that the Church has always considered and avowed, that she was called into existence by the Apostolic agency: and that the teaching of the Apostles was *the cause and not the product* of her faith. It is no less certain, that she has from the first acknowledged and received the canonical books, as being themselves a part, the *written* part, of that Apostolic teaching, that is to say, as being the permanent form of the word by which her faith was first created.

This acknowledgment of the Catholic Church, concerning her own origin and the relation of the Scriptures to it, does in fact dispose of the questions which we often hear debated — whether the Church is before the Bible, or the Bible before the Church — whether the New Testament Scriptures stand upon Christianity, or

1 *Essays and Reviews*, p. 78.

Christianity upon the New Testament Scriptures. It is certain that the Church existed before the Bible, and Christianity before the New Testament Scriptures; but it is also certain that the Church and Christianity derived their own existence from the word which those Scriptures contain. The word was antecedent to the existence of the Church, as the cause is to the effect; the writing of that word, and its reception when written, were subsequent to the formation of the Church, but the writing only made permanent for future time the word by which the Church had been created; and the reception of the writings only recognized them as the same word in its form of permanence. Thus, *while the Church is chronologically before the Bible, the Bible is potentially before the Church;* since the written word, which is the ground of faith to later generations of Christians, is *one* in origin, authority, and substance with the oral word, which was the ground of faith to the first generation of Christians. Any one who pleases may deny this unity of the written and the oral word. I only observe, that, if he does so, he contradicts the "voice of the congregation."

It may further be said, that there is a sense in which some of the New Testament Scriptures are, *as writings*, anterior to Christianity, not only potentially but chronologically. If the ministry of St. Paul was divinely ordained, and used, to develop Christian doctrine, then that ministry was anterior to the full development of Christianity. But his Epistles were part of his ministry, as much a part of it as his spoken word: may we not say a *more* important part, as being, by their character of writing, more deliberate and thorough. It follows that his Epistles are, as really as his oral teaching, chronologically anterior to Christianity as a perfected system. Christianity therefore stands upon the New Testament Scriptures; not the New Testament Scriptures upon Christianity.

LECTURE VI.

NOTE XI., p. 156.

"Epistolicam formam præ libris V. T. habent Scripta N. T. et in his non solum Pauli, Petri, Jacobi, Judæ, sed etiam uterque Lucæ, et omnes Johannis libri. Plus etiam est, quod ipse Dominus Jesus Christus suo nomine septem epistolas dedit, Johannis manu, Apoc. ii. 3, ac tota Apocalypsis instar est epistolæ ab Ipso datæ. Non ad servos, sed ad liberos, eosque emancipatos potissimum, epistolæ mitti sunt solitæ: epistolicumque scribendi genus præ quovis alio accommodatum est ad regnum Dei quam latissime propagandum, et ad animas quam locupletissime ædificandas. Plus in hoc quoque genere unus laboravit Paulus quam ceteri omnes."[1]

NOTE XII., p. 171.

The principle intimated in the text is that the "*perfection*"[2] of Christian doctrine was attained by the reading of the Old Testament in the light of the (elementary) knowledge of Christ; in other words, that the *complete exposition* of the Gospel was the result of a combination of the facts and the words of the old dispensation with the facts and the words of the new, a combination effected in the minds of the Apostles under the teaching of the Holy Ghost, who thus brought to light the meaning and the scope of his own earlier inspirations, preserved in the Law and the Prophets. This method of divine teaching is exhibited in action, and exemplified at length, in the Epistles to the Romans and to the Hebrews. It does in fact constitute and create those two precious writings; which, while they are arguments addressed to others, appear to be also records of the course of thought and formation of opinion in the minds of the writers themselves. They use for the education of other minds the same means and materials which the Holy Ghost had first prepared, and then used, for the education of their own.

1 Bengelii, Gnomon, in Rom. i. 1.

2 τελειότης.

E. g. The mind of St. Paul having received the fundamental principle of justification by grace through faith in Christ, seems to have defined and systematized his doctrine on that subject, by reflection on his own experience of what the Law could do and of what it could not do, on the principle enunciated by Habakkuk, that "the just shall live by his faith," on the fact that Abraham, "being yet uncircumcised, believed God, and it was counted unto him for righteousness," on David's description of "the man to whom the Lord imputeth righteousness without works," &c., &c. The writer to the Hebrews, again, in his penetrating and profound treatment of a multitude of Old Testament texts and of the whole system of the first covenant, not only instructs the disciples whom he addresses, but also incidentally shows in what way their teachers had themselves been taught, namely, by means of the former Scriptures, read in connection with the Gospel facts, and under the teaching of the Holy Ghost.

I do not mean that precisely the same passages which they think fittest for instructing others had been effectual to their own enlightenment, but that they had gained their own perfect light from these and others like them, and that they had themselves been taught through the same medium which they employ. St. Paul's manner of using the Old Testament seems continually to imply his own personal obligations to it.

Some may think that this view of the manner in which the truth was cleared to the minds of its first teachers is inconsistent with, or at least derogatory to, their inspiration; since it implies the processes of study, reflection, comparison, deduction, a gradual increase in the fulness and proportions of their knowledge, and a progress of doctrine in their own minds. Certainly it implies all this, and that is a reason not against, but for its truth; for the Apostolic writings appear to bear witness to such processes and such progress in the minds of their authors. Had it been the purpose of these Lectures to consider the Progress of Doctrine in *this* sense, the view taken of it would have been in accordance with the observation of Bengel, that when the Pauline discourses and writings are placed in chronological order, "a spiritual growth of the Apostle is perceived."[1] Such a view has no kindred with that which has been hazarded by Professor Jowett and others, and which treats the later teaching, not as an expansion, but as a reversal of the earlier; not as a more full and definite, but as an absolutely different doctrine. The doctrine was always one, its full development being implied in its first elements, but, like any other large system of thought, taking time to unfold itself, first in the minds of the teachers, and then in the Church which they taught. The instrument used for this purpose was the Scriptures of the Old Testament. It was so from the very first. When their Lord taught them personally after his resurrection it was through this medium. "He expounded unto them in all the Scriptures the things concerning himself;" "Then opened he their understandings, that they might understand the Scriptures, and said unto them, Thus it is written, and thus it behoved Christ to suffer, and to rise from the dead the third day, and that repentance and remission of sins should be preached in his name among all nations." (Luke xxiv. 27, 45-47.) It is scarcely less evident that the same method was pursued in their subsequent illumination by the Holy Ghost, and that the light which they enjoyed was a light which was reflected from the Scriptures. That which the Lord, before his departure, did by word of mouth, is precisely that which, after his departure, he did by the Holy Ghost; "Then opened he their understandings that they might understand the Scriptures."

There is nothing in this view of the case derogatory to the fulness of their inspiration, for the inspiration in which we believe is not one which in its general action supersedes the natural processes of the mind, but one which mingles itself with them, and insures the truth of their results. In making the former Scriptures the means of enlightening the authors of the later Scriptures, the Holy Spirit established the continuity of his own teaching, and built the Church "upon the foundation of the Apostles and Prophets," amalgamating the two foundations into one. It is from his own experience that St. Paul says to Timothy (albeit not

[1] "*Incrementum* Apostoli spirituale cognoscitur."—Gnomon, Rom. i. 1.

impowered by the Apostolic inspiration), "The Holy Scriptures (of the Old Testament) are able to make thee wise unto salvation (σε σοφίσαι εἰς σωτηρίαν) through faith which is in Jesus Christ." (2 Tim. iii. 15.) The force of the expression lies in the σοφίσαι. The Gospel Timothy has already received; the faith in Christ Jesus he already has; and therefore he is actually in possession of the salvation: but the *wisdom* (σοφία) appertaining to this salvation he is to seek by means of the Scriptures (τὰ δυνάμενα σοφίσαι). This σοφία corresponds to the τελειότης (of doctrine) spoken of in Heb. vi. 1, which is there illustrated by the exquisite example of spiritual exegesis, on the passage "Thou art a priest forever after the order of Melchizedek." Elsewhere, again, the Apostle adverts to this character of his doctrine, "Howbeit we speak wisdom among them that are perfect" (σοφίαν ἐν τοῖς τελείοις, 1 Cor. ii. 6); and there the method of its exposition is described by the remarkable expression (of somewhat doubtful meaning), ἐν διδακτοῖς πνεύματος ἁγίου πνευματικοῖς πνευματικὰ συγκρίνοντες (ver. 13). It seems to me that the interpretation of these words is best derived from the *fact*, everywhere apparent in the Apostle's writings, namely, his habit of working out all the more recondite and (if I may use the word) scientific parts of the Evangelical doctrine by the aid of the Old Testament, the types, images, and sentences of which were, we know, in his sight πνευματικά. Dean Alford's objection to this interpretation, as given by Chrysostom, is founded upon his treatment of the word συγκρίνειν, as if it meant barely to prove or interpret. I think that Chrysostom's illustrations, in the passage referred to, suggest a larger meaning than this; but even the latter of these words, taken in its full sense, would be a more adequate and exact rendering than that which is adopted in its place, "putting together spirituals with spirituals," *i. e. attaching spiritual words* to spiritual things. The συγκρίνειν will more properly represent a *process of thought* and judgment than a mere *method of expression:* it does in fact most aptly represent that process which we actually see in the Epistles, in which the πνευματικά of the old covenant are combined with those of the new in order to establish and elucidate the doctrine which is delivered. The appropriation of the Old Testament *words* to express the New Testament doctrines is a part of this elucidation: *e. g.* the application of the old terms of sacrifice and lustration, to describe the nature of the death and the effect of the blood of Christ.

NOTE XIII., p. 172.

"As Luther complained of the Epistle of James, that it was not occupied with Christ, so in more recent times an inclination has been exhibited to regard James, as he appears to us in his Epistle, as the representative of the faith of the earliest Christians; and hence it has been deduced that the Ebionitic doctrine was the primitive; a conclusion in every respect over-precipitate! For, first, the design of James is such, that it does not fall to him to set forth in order the faith and its contents, but to maintain the πίστις rather according to its ethical significancy, and to contend against all antinomianism. The πίστις he pre-supposes; he does not seek to plant it for the first time; and hence it is incompetent, nay, unjust to him, to treat his Epistle as if he began with the beginning and meant to set forth the fundamental principles of Christianity, which as yet were not in dispute. But, secondly, it would be still more hazardous from this short Epistle — which, according to its avowed design, aims to unfold the ethical and not the dogmatical aspect of Christian truth — to form an estimate of James universally; of whom we have no right, since in other respects he is at one with the synoptic tradition, to assume that in respect to Christological ideas he stands opposed to it. Thirdly, utterly untrue is the assumption that James is to be viewed as the representative of the faith of the earliest Christianity. Rather is his letter, with its polemic against a one-sided faith, an evidence that there was another tendency in the Church, which laid chief stress on faith, not in its ethical purifying power, but viewed principally as an object of knowledge, σοφία; consequently, more in respect of its dogmatic import, and that in a fruitless way, and which held participation in Christianity in this sense for justifying. Over against this theoretical faith he places that which is practical. Still more weighty is what we would adduce fourthly, viz., that it cannot be denied that to the individuality of James the ethical was the most congenial, and hence drew him to give especial effect to the refutation of this false tendency." [1]

Dorner goes on to show that the ethic of St. James is a Christian ethic, and then to point out the actual Christological features of the Epistle. The result is, "that James *had before him the Christian pre-supposition in anthropological and soteriological form*" — a sufficiently alarming sentence, which, however, I print in italics, because it gives the precise point to which I have wished to speak in the text, namely, that a considerate examination of the Epistle shows, that the whole doctrine of the manifestation of Christ in the flesh, and of the mystery of redemption and salvation, is *pre-supposed as already known and accepted* both by the writer and by those to whom he writes. It is this pre-supposition which justifies the place which is assigned to the Epistle in the course of divine instruction.

1 Dorner, on the Person of Christ. Introduction. pp. 62, 63.